Disney by the Numbers

Disney by the Numbers

Facts and Figures
About the Walt Disney World
Theme Parks and Resorts

Anthony M. Caselnova

Theme Park Press
www.ThemeParkPress.com

Theme Park Press publishes its books in a variety of print and electronic formats. Some content that appears in one format may not appear in another.

Editor: Bob McLain
Layout: Artisanal Text

ISBN 978-1-941500-60-6
Printed in the United States of America

Theme Park Press | **www.ThemeParkPress.com**
Address queries to bob@themeparkpress.com

To my parents, Anthony V. and Marie Caselnova, for that first trip to Disney World back in the summer of 1976 that sparked my love for Disney, and to my brothers and sister, Chris Caselnova, Andrew Caselnova, and Jennifer Kreil, for the fun we all had in the back of the station wagon on our Disney trips (and for giving me the entire back seat);

To my two daughters, Lauren and Kristen, who put up with me on all of our Disney trips and let me drag them all over the parks, no matter how tired they were. (Remember that bird at Downtown Disney?);

To all my friends, whether you are old friends from my childhood, or my new and growing Disney family and friends;

And last but not least, you, the reader of this book.

Contents

Publisher's Note

This is not a book of words. It's a book of numbers. Lots and lots of numbers. There are words around the numbers, but it's the numbers that matter.

There isn't a plot. There's minimal structure. The content within each section isn't presented in any particular order. It's all random, even scattershot. You're not meant to read this book; you're meant to wallow in it.

Open the book to any page and you'll be presented with facts and figures—hard data—about different aspects of Walt Disney World. You'll be amazed how many numbers support the pixie dust you enjoy whenever you're at a Disney World park or resort. Without these numbers, there wouldn't be a Walt Disney World.

We all know it started with a mouse. But before the mouse, there were numbers.

Walt Disney World

27,258 acres (about 43 square miles) were purchased by the Disney Company in central Florida for Walt Disney World.

$5,018,770 was the cost to purchase that land.

5,900 acres have been developed.

2,000 acres remain open for development.

1965 is when the public was told about Disney's plans for building a theme park in Florida.

52 months of construction were needed to build the park.

8 million cubic yards of earth were moved.

$4.75 was the cost of a 7-ride book on opening day in 1971.

$5.75 was the cost of a 11-ride book on opening day.

18 months of moving dirt were used to prepare the Magic Kingdom site for construction.

4 colors make up the official colors of Walt Disney World: lagoon blue, mint green, pumpkin orange, lavender.

450 acres is the size of Bay Lake, near the Magic Kingdom.

14.25 pound large-mouth bass is the largest ever caught on Bay Lake, but we'll never know for sure since it is catch-and-release fishing.

4.5 miles of beach line the Seven Seas Lagoon and Bay Lake.

70,000 fingerling bass were originally stocked there.

2.385 billion gallons make up the volume of water that is Bay Lake and the adjoining Seven Seas Lagoon.

14 feet is the depth of Seven Seas Lagoon, but Bay Lake is only 12 feet deep.

14 floats are used in the Electrical Water Pageant that has been featured at the Magic Kingdom since 1971.

1 million cubic yards of earth were dredged from the bottom of the lagoon during the initial excavation phase, with the soil reused for the foundation of the Magic Kingdom. Some of the sand was cleaned and used for nearby beaches.

7 million pens are purchased each year.

14 feet underground is where the utilidors of the Magic Kingdom are located.

9 acres of tunnels make up the utilidors.

4 inches is the distance the driver of the armored car has between its side door and the wall of the utilidors; it the only gas-powered vehicle allowed down there.

2 times a month the horse-shaped hitching posts on Main Street, U.S.A. are scraped and painted.

20 minutes is all it takes to fill Splash Mountain and five minutes to drain it.

7,500 acres were set aside as a conservation area in 1970 with a system of more than 43 miles of canals and 22 miles of levees to control the water level.

100,000 guests is the max capacity for the Magic Kingdom. The parking lot closes at 75,000 to allow room for resort guests arriving by bus, boat, and monorail.

1,000 firework shows per year makes Disney the largest consumer of fireworks in North America.

40,000 couples have married at Disney World, Disneyland, and aboard Disney cruise ships since Disney's Fairy Tale Weddings began in 1991.

70,000 employees are employed by Walt Disney World as of 2015.

$1.8 billion is the annual payroll, with another $1 billion spent on benefits.

9 years is the average tenure of a cast member.

5,000 employees are assigned to maintenance and engineering, including 750 horticulturists and 600 painters.

$100 million is spent each year to maintain the Magic Kingdom.

10 of the 12 monorails can be stored in the maintenance shop on its upper level (the bottom level houses the four steam locomotives that circle the Magic Kingdom). On any given night, two Mark VI monorails are parked outside the gate of the Magic Kingdom. No train will ever be left outside two nights in a row.

72,000 ticket holders at the FedEx Orange Bowl National Championship game in Miami each year receive a surprise free ticket to any Disney theme park in the world. The largest Disney theme park ticket give-away ever was part of the launch of the Happiest Celebration on Earth, celebrating the 50th anniversary of Disneyland and Disney theme parks.

50,000th child to have a Disney theme park wish granted by the Make-A-Wish Foundation and Disney occurred on October 6, 2005.

3,700 different cast member costume designs make up a working wardrobe of about 1.8 million pieces. Approximately 13,000 costume pieces are manufactured each year at Walt Disney World.

1 million yards of fabric are needed to make the costumes.

18 wardrobe-issuing locations are operated by over 500 wardrobe "librarians".

40,000 square feet of wardrobe warehousing are needed to store all the costumes.

160 Disney characters have costumes that cast members wear to meet and greet guests.

90 seamstresses, tailors, and milliners help to produce the costumes at Disney World.

350,000 costume pieces are altered or repaired annually.

200,000 new costumes are manufactured annually.

13 million cast member garments are cleaned annually.

2.5 million garments are in the costuming department.

15 million miles are driven by Disney buses each year.

3,421,399 (approximately) famous "Mouse Ear" hats are sold each year at the parks and resorts.

30th year anniversary for Disney World was celebrated October 1, 2001.

392,040 square feet of space under the Magic Kingdom are used as the utilidors and bustle with activity. Besides navigational information, the walls are covered with motivational information, such as the Seven Rules of a Cast Member.

750 watercraft gives Disney World the 5th largest fleet of watercraft in the world.

150,000 gallons of paint were purchased in 2004, enough to cover 7,500 average-size homes.

110,000 gallons of paint were used by Disney World and its many contractors in 2011.

300 buses transport guests around the resort, making the Disney World fleet the third largest in Florida behind those of Miami and Jacksonville.

194,871 miles of toilet tissue are used annually.

24,409 miles of paper towels are used annually.

337,000 pencils are purchased annually.

148 million sheets of recycled copier paper are used annually.

730,102 gallons of bleach are used annually.

214,000 bandages were provided to guests during 2004.

20,000 different colors of paint are used in Disney World.

290 different outfits are in Mickey's wardrobe closet, including a scuba suit and a tuxedo.

200 different outfits are in Minnie's wardrobe closet, including a cheerleader costume and various evening gowns.

15 million gallons of water are used each day.

5,000+ performers, (not counting the 500 doves that were released) joined in the Grand Opening Celebration of Walt Disney World at the Magic Kingdom on October 25, 1971.

1,076-piece band (including 76 trombones) was led by "Music Man" Meredith Wilson as part of the grand opening parade up Main Street, U.S.A.

500,000 character watches are sold annually, mainly Mickey watches. At any given time, there are more than 200 different varieties of character watches. The most popular timepiece: a gold-tone relief of Mickey Mouse.

210 pairs of sunglasses are turned in every day at the Magic Kingdom lost and found. There have been enough "shades" lost each year in the Magic Kingdom to outfit every resident of Sun City, Arizona; Sun City, California; and Sun City, Florida. Since 1971, an estimated 1.5 million pairs of glasses have found their way into the "lost" bin.

6,000 cell phones are turned in to the lost and found each year.

3,500 digital cameras are turned in.

18,000 hats are turned in.

7,500 autograph books are turned in.

6,000 different types of food are served at Disney World.

350 or more chefs are employed there.

2 times the size of Manhattan Island is the property of Walt Disney World.

1st guest entered Magic Kingdom on October 1, 1971.

50,000,000 guest entered on March 2, 1976.

100,000,000 guest entered on October 22, 1979.

500,000,000 guest entered Disney World on October 13, 1995.

4 million guests have used Disney's Magical Express since the airport shuttle, luggage delivery, and airline check-in service launched May 5, 2005.

250,000 guests ride the various forms of "mass transit" every day, which include monorails, ferryboats, bus services, and water taxis.

100,000 to 200,000 photos of guests are taken each day by Disney's PhotoPass photographers.

4% percent of all amateur photography is estimated to be taken at Walt Disney World and Disneyland.

3 times the park has been closed, once resort wide in September 1999 for Hurricane Floyd; resort wide on September 11, 2001 due to the terror attacks on America; and Epcot only on July 17, 2002, due to a power outage.

72,000 individual Audio-Animatronic functions per second are controlled by the Digital Animation Control System (DACS).

2.2 million travelers were bused from Orlando International Airport to either a Disney resort hotel or cruise ship in 2008, That works out to about $1.6 million a year in payments to the airport.

160 lane miles of paved roads are maintained.

5,500 cast members were employed in October 1971; by the end of the summer of 1972, there were over 10,000 cast members.

56,044 people applied for jobs in 1994; of those 56,044 applicants, 8,750 people became cast members.

2,600 cast members were honored with Distinguished Service Awards in 1996.

850 acres of lakes featuring nearly 130,000 feet of shoreline are on property. And that's just on the surface. Beneath the surface of the seven largest lakes are a combined 3.122 billion gallons of water.

2.385 billion gallons—that's the volume of water in Bay Lake and the adjoining Seven Seas Lagoon, at a combined 596 acres the two largest lakes at Walt Disney World.

8—that's the number of theme park attractions for which guests board boats for a floating adventure: Jungle Cruise, Pirates of the Caribbean, Splash Mountain, Liberty Square Riverboat, it's a small world, Living With the Land, El Rio del Tiempo (River of Time), and Kali River Rapids.

3,000 different job roles are available at Disney World.

52—that's the number of feet of luxurious yacht in Grand 1, available for charter cruises on Seven Seas Lagoon and Bay Lake. The captain and first mate welcome aboard private parties of up to 18 people at the Grand Floridian Marina.

89 varieties of cheese are used by Disney theme parks and resort chefs.

5 adults can sit in a row on the trams.

210 adults can be seated on the trams.

23 trams operate at Disney World.

14 is the number of other theme park attractions, shows, and interactive entertainment during which water plays— or sprays—a memorable role.

13,000 roses decorate the parks and resorts, and many varieties of roses are used.

14 girls were hired to work in the Preview Center when it first opened.

1 million guests were serviced there before it closed.

600 million guests have been to Disney World since it opened in 1971 (as of 2011).

9 screens are required to construct a Circle-Vision theater.

$6.50 was the price of a guided tour on opening day.

01/18/2012—President Barrack Obama made a speech from Main Street, U.S.A. in the Magic Kingdom.

1,500 automated external defoliators (AED) are installed backstage and in guest areas throughout the property.

94 lives have been saved by the AED installed at all Disney properties worldwide as of 2012.

10 million Star Wars light sabers are sold each year.

Magic Kingdom

1967 is when construction on the Magic Kingdom began.

1971 is when the park opened.

$400,000,000.00 was the construction cost.

8,000 employees were working at the Magic Kingdom when it opened.

6 lands are in the Magic Kingdom.

10 million guests visited the park in less than 10 years.

125 acre is the size of the parking lot.

12,156 parking spaces are available.

142 acres of property was used for Magic Kingdom originally.

108 feet is the elevation of the park, according to the sign at the Main Street Railroad Station.

1,100 Audio-Animatronic figures are used. These are all controlled using DACS (Digital Animation Control System) from a central location, along with the 700+ soundtracks for attractions, parades, stores and restaurants.

23 attractions were all you got on opening day.

$3.50 was the admission price on opening day.

$4.95 admission got you an adult 7-ride coupon book that contained a mix of A. B, C, D, E tickets. Additional tickets were $.25 and .50 for each.

100,000 hours and 5,000 yards of fabric were needed by the costumers to create the 125 costumes for the show Cinderellabration.

15 children on average get lost each day and need to be reunited with their parents.

3 horse-drawn street cars are on Main Street, but only 2 run at a time.

10–12 miles per hour is how fast the steam engine trains can speed along the tracks.

1 first aid station is located in the Magic Kingdom near the Crystal Palace.

1 guest information area is located at Town Hall on Main Street, U.S.A.

10 designated smoking areas are in the Magic Kingdom; elsewhere, smoking is prohibited.

5 ATMs are in the park.

1 baby care center is located at the Crystal Place.

8 Nikon picture spots are located in the park.

6 DVC (Disney Vacation Club) locations are there.

60 miles per hour is how fast the trash moves though the Automated Vacuum Assisted Collection System (AVACS).

50 tons a day of trash is handled by AVACS.

3 ferries are used to get from the Ticket and transportation Center (TTC) to the Magic Kingdom. Each ferry is clad in different trim colors and is named for past Disney executives: the General Joe Potter (blue), the Richard F. Irvine (red), and the Admiral Joe Fowler (green).

5 Disneylands can fit in the parking lot of the Magic Kingdom.

100+ hanging baskets are located at the bus turnaround at the park entrance.

2 windows on Main Street are dedicated to Walt. One is at the train station looking over the entrance and the other is at the end of Main Street looking over the park.

1901 was the "year" the emporium opened, and also the year that Walt was born.

3 attractions were unique to Disney World on opening day: Mickey Mouse Revue, Country Bear Jamboree, and the Hall of Presidents.

1.2 million costumes were once stored in the utilidors; in 2005 they were moved to a large facility near cast member parking.

Main Street, U.S.A.

16,742 square feet of retail space stocked with just about anything imaginable in Disney gifts, clothes, and souvenirs can be found in the Emporium on Main Street.

71 is the number on the firehouse (the year the park opened).

4 buildings really exist on Main Street, but have been designed to look like many shops and stores.

7/8 size is how they make the buildings look larger than they really are; they call this forced perspective.

51 building facades on use Cape Cod-style clapboard and gingerbread trim.

850-foot-long Main Street rises about 6 feet from the train station to the castle.

1915 is used on all the Main Street Vehicles; that was the first year Florida started to use license plates.

182 pumpkins are used to decorate Main Street during the Halloween season.

1,026,208 songs have been sung by the Dapper Dans, four notes at a time, since they started singing in 1971.

100-song list is kept by the Dapper Dans, and you can request any song in the list for them to sing.

50 references to Mickey Mouse are in Town Square Theater.

Adventureland
··

Swiss Family Treehouse

1971 is when the Swiss Family Treehouse debuted.

60 feet tall is the height of the treehouse.

90 feet is its diameter.

300,000 leaves are on the treehouse.

42 feet into the ground is the structural support of the Swiss Family Treehouse.

1,400 branches are extend from the treehouse.

9 main branches are on the treehouse.

200 tons is the weight of the treehouse.

300,000 lifelike polyethylene "leaves", which reportedly cost about $1.00 each in 1971, are on the Swiss Family Treehouse.

116 steps must be taken to traverse the treehouse.

500,000 flowers and buds on the treehouse.

300 guests is the maximum capacity.

Magic Carpets of Aladdin

6/14/2000 is when the construction started to build Magic Carpets of Aladdin.

2001 is the year the carpets took flight.

16 "flying" Carpets are on the attraction; each carpet can hold 4 guests.

90 seconds is the total length of the ride.

4 passengers can fly in each carpet.

64 guests can ride at one time.

Enchanted Tiki Room

1971 is when the original Tiki Room Debuted.

1998 is when it was revised.

314 Audio-Animatronics are included in the Tiki Room, including flowers, statues, and birds.

88 singing birds are in the Tiki Room, of course.

9 minutes is the total time of you will spend there.

250 guests can be seated.

1 man voiced all the bird calls and whistles; his name was A. Purvis Pullen.

1 of the Tiki totem poles inside has hidden speakers in or near it, so that if you sit next to it during the show, you can hear certain isolated parts of the music that have been separated into stereo. In particular, you can hear the isolated wooden percussion instruments coming from it during the song "The Tiki Tiki Tiki Tiki Room".

Jungle Cruise

1971 is when the Jungle Cruise debuted.

15 boats are in the fleet of Jungle Cruise ships, each named for an Imagineer that worked on the original attraction: Amazon Annie, Bomokandi Bertha, Congo Connie, Ganges Gertie, Irrawaddy Irma, Mongala Millie, Nile Nelly, Orinoco Ida, Rutshuru Ruby, Sankuru Sadie, Senegal Sal, Ucyali Lolly, Volta Val, Wamba Wanda, Zambesi Zelda.

10 boats can be used at one time.

31 guests can ride each boat.

27-foot-long boats used in the attraction were modeled after the motion picture *The African Queen* starring Humphrey Bogart and Katherine Hepburn.

3.2 mph is the top speed of the boats.

631,000 rounds of ammunition used to be fired on the

Jungle Cruise each year; don't worry, they are just blanks. Now it's an electronic sound effect.

1.75 million gallons of water are held within the attraction.

3 feet deep is the Jungle Cruise river.

14–24 hours are needed to fill the river when it is emptied.

4 rivers of the world are visited by the Jungle Cruise and they are: the Amazon, Nile, Congo, and Mekong.

70 HP CNG engines power the boats.

9 minutes is the total time of the Jungle Cruise.

2000 feet long is the length of its rivers.

Pirates of the Caribbean

1973 is when The Pirates of the Caribbean opened, but it was revised in 2006.

330 guests can ride at one time.

3,600 per hour are the amount of guests that can go though Pirates of the Caribbean.

15-18 guests per boat can ride.

220 audio speakers have been replaced throughout the attraction.

3 bass subwoofers have been installed within the "battle scene" between the pirate galleon and the Spanish fortress to provide a sense of concussion during the firing of the cannons.

400 Disney Imagineers have been working in California and Florida on the research, planning, and installation of the enhancements to Pirates of the Caribbean.

25 million people are estimated to visit Pirates.

23 adults can sit in each boat split across 6 rows.

27 boats are used.

750,000 million gallons of water flow though Pirates of the Caribbean.

18,000 gallons of water are pumped though each minute at a minimum.

20,000 gallons of water are pumped though each minute at a maximum.

8.5 minutes will be the time of your journey through Pirates.

65 Audio-Animatronics pirates and villagers are used.

60 Audio-Animatronics animals and birds are used.

14-foot drop awaits you in the Pirates of the Caribbean.

4 cannons are on the roof of the attraction.

15 cannons are located inside.

Frontierland

Big Thunder Mountain Railroad

1980 is when Big Thunder Mountain debuted.

2,780 feet of track was laid.

197 feet tall is Big Thunder.

2.5 acre is the total acreage used.

6,500 tons of steel beams, rods, and mesh were used to construct the attraction.

4,675 tons of concrete were used.

90,000 gallons of water were used.

4,000 gallons of dessert paint were used.

150 guests can ride at one time.

30 people can fit in each train, with 5 cars per train and 6 guests per car.

$17 million was the total construction costs of Big Thunder

Mountain Railroad in 1979. $300,000.00 of that money was spent on authentic props and decorations alone.

6 trains on the ride are named *I.M. Brave*, *I.M. Fearless*, *I.B. Hearty*, *U.B. Bold*, *U.R. Daring*, and *U.R. Courageous*.

5 trains can run simultaneously.

3 minutes and 30 seconds is the ride time.

20 Audio Audio-Animatronics can be seen.

3 drops are on Big Thunder Mountain.

3 lifts are on it, too.

25 miles per hour is the maximum speed for this train.

25% larger is this Big Thunder than Disneyland's version.

50 feet is the height of the track.

Country Bear Jamboree

1971 is when Country Bear Jamboree debuted.

20 Audio-Animatronics perform in the show.

380 guests is the maximum capacity that can watch the Jamboree at once.

18 bears are on hand to perform.

1st attraction to make its world debut at Walt Disney World was the Country Bear Jamboree.

5 other animals are in the show: a raccoon, a buffalo, a stag, a moose, and a skunk!.

Splash Mountain

1992 is the year Splash Mountain debuted.

86 feet down at a 45-degree angle decent is the thrill in this thrill ride.

40 mph is the top speed you'll travel, which is faster than on Space Mountain.

9.2 acres were consumed for Splash Mountain, which is approximately 4.5 times bigger than Disneyland's 2.03 acres version of the ride.

440 guests can ride at one time.

2,600 feet long, or about 1/2 a mile, is the length of the concrete flume.

36-feet long and 22-feet high is the showboat in the final scene.

28,000 gallons of water are pushed though Splash Mountain each minute.

5 minutes is all it takes to drain the entire flume system.

20 minutes is all it takes to fill it (with 965,000 gallons of water).

956,000 gallons of water are recycled every 4 minutes.

1 million gallons of water are held in a backstage reservoir, which is 50 feet deep by 60 feet by 60 feet.

6 water pumps feed the 2 zones of Splash Mountain.

4 of the 6 water pumps are used; the other 2 are back-ups.

2 feet diameter is the size of the tubes carting water through the water pumps.

2 computers run all the controls.

36 hidden cameras are on Splash Mountain, monitored at all times by cast members.

15 exit doors are located throughout the attraction (many of which aren't seen by guests).

5 drops are at Splash Mountain.

3 lifts are there, too.

$1.3 million dollars was the cost for the hopping Br'er Rabbit.

60 logs are at Splash Mountain.

1 ton is the dead load of each log.

50 logs can be run at one time.

8 guests can fit in each log.

103 Audio-Animatronics are used.

3 times is the amount of times Prince William, Prince Harry, and Princess Diana rode Splash Mountain, their favorite ride, in 1993.

Tom Sawyer Island

1973 is when Tom Sawyer Island debuted.

3 wooden rafts to Tom Sawyer Island are named after characters in Mark Twain's novel, *The Adventures of Tom Sawyer*: Tom Sawyer, Injun Joe, and Becky Thatcher.

70 People can ride on each raft to Tom Sawyer Island.

400 guests can be on the Tom Sawyer Island at one time.

6 paintbrushes were once hidden each day on Tom Sayer Island; if you found one and brought it to a cast member, you received a prize.

Frontierland Shootin' Arcade

1971 is when the Frontierland Shootin' Arcade debuted.

5 minutes is how long the fun lasts.

16 guns are at the Frontierland Shootin' Arcade.

97 different targets are there to shoot at, and the landscape includes a bank, jail, hotel and cemetery.

54 caliber Hawkins rifles are used.

2,000 gallons of paint are needed each year to repaint the targets.

Fantasyland
....

Cinderella Castle

189 feet to the highest point on Cinderella Castle, which can be seen as far as 2 miles away at the Ticket and transportation Center.

3,727 towers are on the castle. They were pre-fabricated near the site, then slated, gilded, and hoisted into place.

29 towers were in the original design, but 2 were deleted during construction.

13 gargoyles are on the exterior.

40 coats of arms are on display inside Cinderella's Royal Table restaurant. Each refers to someone who played a significant role in the heritage and history of the Disney company.

18 months were need to construct the castle.

500,000 bits of glass in 500 different colors are used inside the castle.

1 mile away is the distance the castle is designed to be seen from.

13 intricately carved, winged gargoyles appear on the exterior.

600 tons of steel went into the construction of the castle, and not a single stone.

1996-97, to celebrate Walt Disney World's 25th anniversary, the castle was transformed into a huge "cake" with large decorations and more than 400 gallons of pink paint.

25 candles adorned the cake.

1 day is the number of times the castle was vandalized with toilet paper and graffiti to commemorate the opening of Stitch's Great Escape.

3 elevators are inside the castle.

5 tile mosaics designed by Imagineer Dorothea Redmond tell the story of Cinderella just inside the castle breezeway. Each of the panel tile mosaics is 15 feet high and 10 feet wide.

5 murals contain about 500 colors and 1 million pieces of glass, many of them fused with real silver and 14-karat gold. Smooth-faced Venetian glass and rough-surfaced smalti (enameled or glazed glass) traditionally used by Italian craftsman were incorporated into the design.

6 artists worked more than 2 years to complete the murals in the archway of Cinderella Castle.

300,000 pieces of glass were used to make the interior murals.

30,000 pictures are taken of Cinderella Castle everyday.

18 towers and spires are topped with sparkling gold-painted finials.

Cinderella Castle Suite

2 years were need to construct the mosaic panels by artist Hanns-Joachim Scharff and his team.

30,000 tiles are on the Cinderella's coach mosaic tile floor.

3,400 pieces of 24-carat gold and more than 120 white-gold pieces were used on the floor.

4 months of hand-cut work by 4 craftswomen who share more than 100 years of experience working with mosaics were used to create the mosaic floor.

3 hand-woven rugs from Thailand are in the bedchamber.

2 authentic antique "slipper" chairs are there. They look like children's furniture, but were actually used during the 17th and 18th century by adults who sat in the chairs to put shoes on.

2 custom-designed headboards stand 8'2" tall with a "C" (for Cinderella) crest.

600-pound antique limestone fireplace is in the suite. The 17th century Gothic fireplace is molded from an original wood fireplace from France. The fiber optics gives the appearance of a fire with glowing embers.

2 cinder pots reflect Cinderella's humble roots. They are made from hand-hammered copper, with French reproduction, red with gold accents.

3 mosaics contain a total of 30,000 tiles made of Italian smalti glass, hand-cut and placed by Disney artisans. Features include a crystal slipper, a crystal pumpkin, the initials "WD" (Walt Disney), and a mouse looking up toward the castle.

Prince Charming Regal Carrousel

1971 is when Prince Charming Regal Carrousel debuted.

86 horses gallop on the carrousel.

6 chariots are available if you don't want to ride a horse.

91 guests can ride the carrousel.

2 minutes is all you get.

26 classic Disney tunes play in the background.

7 miles per hour is how fast the horses on the outside move.

2,325 lights are on the carrousel.

1 horse has a golden tooth, which is copied after Lillian Disney's horse.

1 horse has a golden ribbon on its tail.

1 is the number of times the carrousel has been moved. While the Magic Kingdom was being built Roy Disney noticed that the carrousel was off center when seen through Cinderella's castle, and it was quickly moved to the proper position.

18 hand-painted scenes adorn the canopy.

0 is the number of identical horses. Each horse has its own color palette as well as its own unique number on the bridal.

1917 was when the carrousel was built, making it the oldest attraction in Walt Disney World.

90 carousels were made by Philadelphia Toboggan Company (though a small number are likely refurbishments of existing carousels) and Prince Charming Regal Carrousel is number 46.

Dumbo the Flying Elephant

1971 is when Dumbo debuted in Fantasyland.

1993 is when it was refurbished.

32 elephant ride vehicles are on Dumbo.

64 guests can ride at one time.

10 elephant ride vehicles were on the original version of Dumbo.

1 minute and 30 seconds is the length of the ride.

It's a Small World

1971 is when It's a Small World debuted.

2006 is when it was refurbished.

10 minutes and 20 seconds is the total ride time.

1964–5 New York World's Fair is when, where, and why Walt Disney created the attraction.

289 dolls were in Small World when it opened in 1971, representing 5 continents and singing in 5 languages (English, Italian, Japanese, Spanish, Swedish).

553 Audio-Animatronics figures are in the attraction, which include not only the kids, but the animals as well.

22 different languages are used to say the word "Goodbye", which is written on the wall as the ride comes to an end.

6 distinct rooms are in the attraction. The first is the loading/unloading area, then the European room, the Far East room, the African room, the islands of the Pacific room, and the "white room" celebrating children of all cultures.

5th room is the only room where the theme song is not sung.

6th room is where every doll is dressed in white.

1,085-foot long canal in the ride is called Seven Seaways.

500,000 gallons of water is used to fill the canal.

2,296 garments are worn by the dolls.

4 types of Americans are represented in Small World: cowboy, Hawaiian, Inuit, and Native American.

30 boats can run simultaneously.

20 guests can fit per boat, though that would be unusually crowded.

147 toys are in the attraction.

36 animated props are there, too.

100 nations are represented by all the different dolls.

14 times the word "world" is sung in the theme song.

5 different versions of It's a Small World exist in the different Disney theme parks worldwide.

Mad Tea Party

1971 is when the Mad Tea Party debuted.

18 teacups are on the attraction.

4 guests can ride in each tea cup.

72 guests can ride each time.

10/6 on the Mad Hatter's hat is the price of the hat: ten shillings, 6 pence.

2 minutes is the total ride time.

The Barnstormer

1996 is when the Barnstormer debuted.

1 minute and 30 seconds is the total ride time.

32 guests can ride the Barnstormer at once.

2 trains run at the same time.

8 cars are on each train.

30 feet is the total height.

20 miles per hour is the top speed of the Barnstormer.

1 lift is all you get.

The Many Adventures of Winnie the Pooh

1999 is when The Many Adventures of Winnie the Pooh debuted.

4 guests can fit in each "honey pot" on the attraction.

48 guests can ride at the same time.

12 honey pots are on the ride at once.

3 minutes is the total ride time.

Mickey's PhilharMagic

2003 is when Mickey's PhilharMagic debuted.

150-foot wide and 28 feet high screen is used in Mickey's PhilharMagic. It is the largest seamless projection screen in the world.

12 minute 3D show is the length of the show.

486 guests can be seated and there is space for 10 wheelchairs.

8 scenes are in the show: PhilharMagic Stage, Be Our Guest, Sorcerer's Apprentice, Part of Your World, I Just Can't Wait To Be King, You Can Fly, A Whole New World, and the Finale.

6 theater effects are used: water, air jets, fog, apple pie scent, jasmine scent, and light effects.

4 different attractions have been at this location.

Peter Pan's Flight

1971 is the year Peter Pan's Flight debuted.

3 minutes of flight is all Peter Pan can deliver.

2 guests can ride in 1 ride vehicle.

60 guests can ride at once.

Be Our Guest Restaurant

3 dining rooms are in Be Our Guest.

550 guests can dine at the same time.

300 tables are located in the restaurant.

3 chandeliers hang in the dinning room.

2'-tall by 11 ½-feet wide is the size of the largest chandelier.

84 candles can be found on the center chandelier.

100 large crystals can be found there, too.

Under the Sea ~ Journey of The Little Mermaid

1st Disney ride-through attraction that takes you "under the sea" with Ariel, Prince Eric, Sebastian, and Ursula, with music and scenes from *The Little Mermaid* film.

200 Audio-Animatronics figures perform.

128 figures are visible in the ride.

50 spinning starfish are in the "Under the Sea" scene.

86-foot long hand-painted mural greets guests in the loading area.

7.5 feet tall is the height of Ursula.

12 feet wide is her width.

6 frolicking mermaids and King Triton can be seen on the exterior of the building. The mermaids are Ariel's older sisters: Aquata, Andrina, Arista, Attina, Adella, and Alana.

5½ minutes is the total ride time.

4 songs from the movie are played during the ride: "Part of Your World," "Kiss the Girl," "Poor Unfortunate Souls," and "Under the Sea".

1st the Imagineers built a 1/4inch scale model and then as a 1-inch scale model so they could "ride" through the attraction scene-by-scene before full construction began.

11/15/1989 is when the *The Little Mermaid* won Academy Awards for Best Song, "Under the Sea", and Best Original Score.

1st Disney film based on a classic fairy tale since *Sleeping Beauty* three decades earlier.

Liberty Square

500 young trees have been brought to life by the "Liberty Oak", which is the focal point in Liberty Square. It all started with a harvested acorn.

130-year-old live oak tree (*Quercus virginiana*) was found on the eastern part of the Disney property in 1971 and moved about 8 miles to the Magic Kingdom.

38 tons was the weight of the tree when they first moved it.

18' by 16' by 4' deep was the size of the root ball.

13 lanterns hang from the tree, representing the original 13 colonies of the United States.

Hall Of Presidents

1971 is the year the Hall of Presidents debuted.

47 different body functions and 15 hand and facial motions are what President Lincoln can manage.

700 people can be seated in the Hall of Presidents.

20 minutes is the total show time.

6 months is how long it takes to install a newly elected president.

130 new images were ultimately woven into the show, as the Imagineering team combed through the National Archives, Library of Congress, museums, and private collections to acquire them.

220 years of history are presented in 25 minutes. The "cavalcade of U.S. history" that Walt Disney originally envisioned remains key to the 25-minute show, with the rewritten story transcending the events by bringing into full focus the bond between the people and the chief executives that have guided America through its challenges.

3 presidents are programmed to speak to guests in the updated show: George Washington, Abraham Lincoln, and Barack Obama.

3 screens (each 30' by 18') are used for the show.

70mm film was used for the original opening movie, but now the movie is projected in high-definition video.

Haunted Mansion

1971 is when The Haunted Mansion debuted.

320 guests can ride through the mansion at one time.

4 stories tall is the height of the mansion, with two separate wings, as well as a bell tower and a conservatory.

5 pound bags of theatrical dust, known as "Fuller's Earth", is used to decorate the 200 props at the Haunted Mansion. It's rumored that enough dust has been used since the attraction's opening in 1971 to bury the mansion completely.

999 Happy Haunts are contained in the Haunted Mansion, though only 107 of them are represented by Audio-Animatronics figures.

2 living figures are also present, but not in the mansion itself: the caretaker Dick O'Dell and his dog.

160 OmniMover ("Doom Buggy") ride vehicles operate at a brisk 1.4 mph.

3,200 guests per hour can be accommodated in mansion.

11 minutes is the total ride time.

960 feet of track are included in the mansion.

5 singing busts in the graveyard scene warble the attraction's theme song, "Grim Grinning Ghosts". Though sometimes mistaken for Walt Disney, the face on the bust farthest to the left is that of Thurl Ravenscroft, the song's soloist. Ravenscroft is known to millions of fans as the voice of Tony the Tiger, the mascot of Kellogg's Frosted Flakes cereal.

13 candles are on the birthday cake in the dining room scene.

4 paintings are on the walls of the stretching room.

8 styles of the song "Grim Grinning Ghosts" can be heard.

200 objects can be found in the attic, including musical instruments and nautical artifacts.

Liberty Square Riverboat

1971 is the year the Liberty Square Riverboats debuted.

1973 is when a new riverboat was put into service.

9 feet deep is the depth of the Rivers of America. How does the Liberty Belle float and traverse such shallow water? It rides along a rail attached to the riverbed below.

400 guests can ride the steam-wheel paddleboat named the *Richard F. Irvine* which was the 1st boat built at the Walt Disney World on-site metal shop.

15 minutes is the length of the trip around Tom Sawyer Island on the Rivers of America.

700 degrees is the temperature of the riverboat's boiler.

1 steam engine powers everything on the riverboat, including lights and sounds.

113 feet long is the length of the riverboat.

26 feet is its width.

46 feet tall is its height.

1 smokestack is on the *Irvine*, which is different than the *Fowler* and *Twain* riverboats.

6 months were needed to construct the original riverboat, the *Irvine*, on Disney World property.

280-horsepower piston engine powers the steam-driven riverboat.

Tomorrowland

Astro Orbiter

1974 is when Astro Orbiter debuted as Star Jets.

1994 is when the Astro Orbiter was refurbished.

11 revolutions per minute are all the Astro Orbiter does, even though it seems like more.

12 vehicles are on the Astro Orbiter.

2 guests can ride in each rocket.

24 guests can be in orbit at one time.

90 seconds is your total flight time.

40 feet is the radius of each arm on the Astro Orbiter.

1.2 million miles are traveled per year on the ride.

50 feet in height, it towers over Tomorrowland.

3/4 of a mile is the total distance you travel on your short journey.

2011 was when the attraction closed for the day due to a fire in a light fixture.

Buzz Lightyear Space Ranger Spin

1998 is when Buzz Lightyear's Space Ranger Spin debuted.

900,000 to 999,999 points are needed to become a Galactic Hero.

10 interactive scenes are where you do all your shooting.

4 minutes and 30 seconds is the length of the ride.

2 guests can ride in each ride vehicle, and each guest has his own space gun.

4 different shaped targets are available: round, square, triangle, and diamond. The triangle- and diamond shaped targets are worth the most points.

201 guests can ride Buzz Lightyear Space Ranger Spin at once.

3 colors are used in the queue: white, bright blue, and chartreuse.

Monsters, Inc. Laugh Floor

2007 is when Laugh Floor debuted.

15 minutes is the length of each show.

460 guests can be seated inside the comedy club.

Space Mountain

1975 is when Space Mountain debuted.

15 two-car trains are used in the attraction, with up to 13 in use at one time.

2 rockets are on each train

30 rockets are numbered 1 to 31; there is no number 13 rocket.

6 guests can sit in each rocket.

2 rockets are on each train.

180 guests can ride at once.

28 mph is the speed of the rockets.

183 feet is the height to the top of Space Mountain.

39-degree drop is the steepest descent.

35-foot drop is the last one on the ride.

3,196 feet is the length of the left-side alpha track.

3,186 feet is the length of the right-side omega track. The alpha track crosses over the omega track, hence the difference in length.

4 tracks were originally called for when the attraction was in the concept stage.

900–1200 guests can ride Space Mountain per hour.

2500 guests can ride Space Mountain per hour if both tracks are operating.

2 minutes and 30 seconds is the total ride time.

4,508,500 cubic feet are contained inside the mountain.

300 feet is its base diameter.

3 years of construction were needed to build Space Mountain.

72 massive pre-stressed concrete beams form the gigantic sealed cone.

5,300 tons is the weight of the concrete beams. They were cast near the Space Mountain site and then hoisted into place by mammoth cranes to complete the cone.

117 feet is the length of each beam.

13' wide at the bottom and 4' wide at the top are the dimensions of each beam.

300-foot diameter building encloses Space Mountain.

15 feet of Space Mountain is sunk below ground.

10 years to develop and more than two years to actually construct is how long it took to bring the attraction to life.

2 acres is the inside area.

72,500 square feet is the size of the building.

50,000 balloons were released when Space Mountain opened on January 15, 1975.

2,000 piece band played on that day.

Stitch's Great Escape

2004 is when Stitch's Great Escape debuted.

39 inches tall does not make Stitch all that dangerous, but he can perform 48 different functions.

18 minutes is the time of the show.

1,600 pounds is the combined weight of the laser cannons in Stitch's Great Escape.

240 guests can be seated in 2 different theaters.

Tomorrowland Transit Authority (TTA)

1975 is when the TTA debuted as the WEDway PeopleMover.

1996 is when the WEDway PeopleMover was refurbished and renamed the TTA.

35 5-car trains can be used on the TTA, though 30 is the maximum run simultaneously.

4 adults can ride in one car.

5 cars are in each train.

10 minutes is your ride time.

533 electromagnets generating an effect called linear induction are used on the TTA.

5,484 feet is the length of the tracks.

6.84 miles per hour is the top speed of a car.

1.84 miles per hour is the speed of the TTA platform.

629 motors can be found on the TTA.

7 station announcements are made during your 10 minute journey.

Walt Disney's Carousel of Progress

1964 is when Walt Disney's Carousel of Progress debuted at the New York World's Fair. After the fair, it was moved to Disneyland in 1967, and then to Disney World in 1975.

6 theaters appear on Carousel of Progress.

240 guests per theater can "ride" during each show.

2 feet per second is how fast the audience moves from show room to show room.

20 minutes and 45 seconds is the length of the show.

8 Audio-Animatronics figures in 4 scenes (for a total of 32 figures) are seen.

375 tons is the gross weight of the attraction.

Tomorrowland Speedway

1971 is when Tomorrowland Speedway debuted, as the Grand Prix Raceway.

1996 is when the ride was refurbished.

146 cars are used at one time.

2 guests can ride in each car.

292 guests can ride at once.

5 minutes is the ride time, depending on traffic.

2,260 feet of track are laid at the Tomorrowland Speedway.

9-horsepower engines give a maximum car speed of 7.5 mph.

$6000 was the cost of each car. The gas-powered car has disc brakes, rack-and-pinion steering, but no brake pedal.

1909 bricks from the Indianapolis Speedway are embedded in the starting line between lanes 2 and 3 close to the elevated walkway.

Parades, Shows, Entertainment

Festival of Fantasy

100 cast members participate in the parade.

12 Disney stories and Disney characters are represented among the parade floats.

9 parade floats are used.

40 additional characters are presented in animated or sculpted form.

50 feet long is the Princess Garden lead float.

28 feet above the float is the Jolly Roger.

32 feet tall is Mickey's Airship finale float (it's the tallest float).

90 feet long are the final 3 floats of there parade.

10 different costume houses were used in 8 cities and 2 countries.

27 separate custom0designed fabrics were created by Mirena Rada in collaboration with graphic artist Paul Jordan, from Creative Costuming.

28 separate fabrics are used to make up one Swing Thug #1 costume (*Tangled* unit). His vest requires vinyl to be cut into 75 separate diamond shapes and then stitched onto fabric.

30 yards of fabric are used to make one Seashell Girl costume, which includes 12 different colors of Nitex Mesh.

3 separate colors are used in the coral pieces for the Coral Twins (*The Little Mermaid* unit) and baked and finished for 16 hours each in an oven.

95 gold lamé dots are used on Minnie Mouse's dress and hat (finale unit).

3 separate clown wigs are used on the Bubble Girl (finale unit) headpiece.

148 yards of horsehair are used to make the Cha Cha Girl (finale unit). Her wig was designed with 4 colors, and then rolled, pressed, and curled by hand.

53 feet from snout to tail is the size of the Steampunk-inspired Maleficent Dragon; it reaches 26 feet in the air.

Wishes

10/09/2003 is when Wishes debuted.

12 minutes is the length of this fireworks show.

7/4/1985 is when Tinker Bell took her first flight during Wishes.

105 pounds is the weight limit for Tinker Bell.

5'3" is the height limit for Tinker Bell.

11 locations around the Magic Kingdom are used as launching sites for the fireworks.

557 firework-firing cues are used.

683 individual pieces of pyrotechnics are used.

15 songs from 10 classic Disney animated features are played: *Snow White and the Seven Dwarfs* (1937), *Pinocchio* (1940), *Fantasia* (1940), *Cinderella* (1950), *Peter Pan* (1953), *Sleeping Beauty* (1959), *The Little Mermaid* (1989), *Beauty and the Beast* (1991), *Aladdin* (1992), and *Hercules* (1997).

Mickey's Very Merry Christmas Party

300,000 cookies are consumed each night of the party.

1,200 gallons of hot cocoa are drunk each night, too.

5,500 lights are hung on each icon Christmas tree in each park or resort for the holidays.

70-ton crane is used to position the theme park Christmas trees into place each year.

1,500 decorated Christmas trees are placed throughout Disney World.

8.5 million lights are hung.

15 miles of garland are used.

300,000 yards of ribbon are used.

164 cast members perform in Mickey's Once Upon a Christmastime Parade.

Main Street Electrical Parade.

1977 is when the Main Street Electrical Parade debuted.

26 units portraying 9 themes are in the parade.

575,000 lights in six colors (amber, blue, chartreuse, green, pink, red) are used. Amber (152,000) is the most common.

27 tons of batteries power the lights, audio, and float movement (enough power to light 32 homes).

550 miles of wiring were need for the parade.

530,000 bulbs were required to light the parade.

23 illuminated floats are in the 2010 edition of the Main Street Electrical Parade.

2 classics will return to the lineup after a 13-year hiatus: the shimmering diamond mine of Snow White and the Seven Dwarfs, and the Pleasure Island haunts of Pinocchio.

600,000 lights will twinkle in this edition of the parade.

10,000 are new "pixie dust" lights spread over the 23 parade floats.

25,000 points of light (75% powered by an LED source) are on the Tinker Bell float alone.

160 dimmers are on the Tinker Bell float as part of a new control system makes it possible for each light to be programmed individually.

80 performers appear in each presentation of the parade.

11,000 lights are on the dancers' costumes alone. Thanks to the energy-efficient LED lights, some of the dancers' costumes now carry only one battery pack instead of two.

500 batteries supply power for lighting, propulsion, audio, and special effects this version of the parade.

5 miles of wire is used throughout the floats.

18' 6" tall is the Clock tower float, the tallest in the parade.

7 cars that span 118 feet is the length of the finale "Fireworks" float, the longest in the parade.

3500 feet is the length of green LED strings used to create the leaf fields on the new Tinker Bell float.

5,600 pounds is the gross weight of the Elliot the dragon float.

16 feet tall is the height of Elliot.

10 feet wide is the width.

The Electrical Water Pageant

10/24/1971 is when the Electrical Water Pageant debuted.

14 floats are used in the pageant.

25 feet tall is the height of the floats.

1 generator is on each float.

800-watt sound system is used to play the pageant music.

Mickey's Not-So-Scary Halloween Party

5 days are needed to install the fall overlay in the Magic Kingdom.

216 tons of candy are given out to trick or treaters during the party nights.

35 different varieties of candy are available.

1/2 million pounds of candy and healthy treats are given out during the 10 nights of the party.

20 tractor-trailers were used to ship all the candy in 2011.

Celebrate The Magic

16 projectors are used to project images on Cinderella Castle during the show.

4 locations are used to house the 16 projectors.

10 minutes is the length of the show.

500 images are used from same-day guests.

5,000 images are displayed each night during the 10-minute show.

Magic Kingdom Extinct Attractions, Shows, and Parades

If You Could Fly

1987 is when If You Could Fly debuted.

1989 is when it was retired.

If You Had Wings

102 ocean-blue OmniMover vehicles were used in the extinct If You Had Wings attraction, which closed in June 1, 1987.

Delta Dreamflight

1989 is when Delta Dream Flight Debuted.

1995 is when it was retired.

5 minutes was the ride time.

2 guests could sit in each ride vehicle.

20,000 Leagues Under the Sea

1971 is when 20,000 Leagues Under the Sea debuted.

1996 is when it was retired.

11.5 million gallons of water were in the tank.

38-passenger (39 counting the cast member "captain") submarines were used, each called *Nautilus* and distinguished by the Roman numeral markings on their exteriors.

61 feet was the length of each submarine.

58 tons was the weight.

Mr. Toads Wild Ride

1971 is when Mr. Toads Wild Ride debuted.

1998 is when it was retired.

2 minutes was the time of the ride.

Extra TERRORestrial Alien Encounter

162 people could be seated per show.

18 minutes was the time of the ride.

48" height requirement and minimum age of 7 were required, due to the fright factor.

Snow White's Scary Adventures

1971 is when Snow White's Scary Adventures debuted.

1994 is when it was refurbished.

4 guests could ride in one vehicle.

66 guests can ride the attraction at once.

3 minutes is the ride time.

Mickey's Toontown Fair

7th land in Magic Kingdom is Toontown; it was the only one added to the original park layout.

1988 was when Mickey's Birthdayland was opened for Mickey's 60th birthday and eventually became Mickey's Toontown Fair.

Donald's Boat

1996 is when Donald's Boat debuted.

60 guests could ride Donald's boat at once.

Mickey's Country House

1998 is when Mickey's Country House came to town.

2,100 props were purchased.

985 props were made from scratch by Imagineering.

125 guests could go through Mickey's house at one time.

Minnie's Country House

1996 is when Minnie's Country House came to town.

0 is the number of bedrooms in Minnie's house.

125 guests can be in Minnie's House at one time.

Epcot

1979 is when construction on Epcot began.

1982 is when the park opened.

3 years were needed to constructed Epcot; it was the largest construction project in the world at that time.

3,000 designers were used to create Epcot.

22 construction companies were used.

500 sub-contractors were needed.

10,000 construction workers were employed.

54 million cubic feet of dirt was moved.

300 acres, the size of Epcot, is almost triple the size of the Magic Kingdom.

162 acres of parking lots exist for Epcot.

12,155 parking spaces are available.

1.4 billion dollars was the estimated cost to build Epcot, though the budget was only $600 million.

19 major design revisions are what Epcot went through on its way to the final design.

$1.4 billion was the approximate cost for the original construction of Epcot.

1.2 miles tall is how tall the golfer would have to be if Spaceship Earth were a golf ball. The hole would have to be 417 feet in diameter.

1.24 miles is the circumference of the World Showcase lagoon.

4,000 construction workers were needed to complete "Phase 1" of the Epcot theme park.

19,000 square feet is the size of Mouse Gear, the largest retail store in any theme park; it occupies the space once used for the Epcot Discovery Center and the Epcot Poll Theater.

3.5 acres of flowers and plants are at Epcot.

70 acres of lawn are there.

12,500 specimens of trees are planted at Epcot.

100,000 shrubs, too

300 optical, motion, and sound effects are used at the park, which is more than 5 times the number used at the Magic Kingdom.

274 continuous special effects are used.

250 advanced projection systems are used to produce special effects.

190,000 feet (35 miles) of electrical wire and 22,000 feet (4 miles) of conduit are in the park.

750,000 images can be stored on the "Leave a Legacy" monoliths when it is completely filled. Each stone is 3'–19' tall and can weigh as much as 50,000 pounds.

257 feet tall, the Millennium 2000 Icon was the tallest point at Walt Disney World, besting the 199 feet of The Twilight Zone Tower of Terror at Disney-MGM Studios.

$367,635,927.00 is the taxable value of the Epcot property.

$110,680,500.00 is its land value.

$243,137,355.00 is its building value.

$5,150,667.56 is the taxes paid in 2006.

20,000 residents were to live in this Experimental Prototype Community of Tomorrow.

3 water fountains make submarine sounds, sing opera, or make wisecracks when you turn on the water.

28 discoveries and inventions are honored in the Epcot Inventors Circle.

3 films in its history have been shown at Epcot's Magic Eye Theater: *Magic Journeys*, *Captain EO*, and *Honey, I Shrunk the Audience*.

4,500 buildings were in the original Epcot community plan.

500 million board feet of lumber became props at Epcot.

Future World

Circle of Life

1995 is the year Circle of Life debuted at The Land.

19 minutes and 20 seconds is the length of the show.

428 people can see Circle of Life show per performance.

Universe of Energy

1982 is when the Universe of Energy debuted.

2 acres were used to build the attraction.

30,000 pounds is the weight of the moving theater which is guided by a $1/8^{th}$-inch thick wire embedded in the floor. The vehicles detect the wire and follow it along the ride path.

220-degree screen stretches across the theater.

15% of the power needed to run the Universe of Energy comes from the photo-voltaic cells on the roof. There are 80,000 cells, producing a peak output of about 70,000 watts of direct current, which is then converted into alternating current.

30,000 pounds is the weight of the ride vehicles.

96 guests can ride the Universe of Energy at once.

32 feet high and 515 feet long are the dimensions of the primeval diorama.

5,700 hours were spent by the artists to paint this diorama.

70mm projection screen measuring 157 feet wide by 32 feet high is in theater 1 of the Universe of Energy.

2 attractions have occupied this pavilion.

26 Audio-Animatronics are in the Universe of Energy.

Ellen's Energy Adventure

1996 is when Ellen's Energy Adventure debuted.

6 untracked ride vehicles are used.

96 guests can ride in each vehicle.

582 guests can ride Ellen's Energy Adventure at once.

45 minutes is the length of the attraction.

1 Audio-Animatronic of Ellen DeGeneres is all that appears.

Journey into Imagination with Figment

1993 is when Journey into Imagination with Figment debuted.

80-foot upside down waterfall is on display outside the Imagination pavilion.

7 guests can ride in each vehicle.

1,776 guests can fit in the theater of Journey into Imagination with Figment.

13 minutes is the length of the ride.

78 out of the 200 special effect patents created for the original Epcot Center were used in this attraction.

Living with the Land

1982 is when Living with the Land debuted.

20 people can fit on each boat.

20 boats operate at the same time.

6 acres is consumed by the Land pavilion, making it the largest pavilion in Epcot.

3,000 square feet is covered by the colorful tile mosaic at the entrance to the Land.

150,000 individually cut and shaped pieces of tile took 3 months to install on the mosaic mural at the Land.

14 minutes is the length of the ride.

134 feet long with 150,000 individually shaped pieces of marble, granite, slate, glass and gold to represent the layers of the Earth lead to the Great Hall at The Land pavilion.

5 balloons hang here. The middle one represents Earth, and four around it represent the seasons: yellow for summer, orange for fall, blue for winter, and green for spring.

36-38 guests per boat can ride on Living with the Land.

2,736 guests can ride per hour.

60-foot-high dome is located in The Land.

6 acres in size makes The Land as large as all of Tomorrowland in the Magic Kingdom.

30 tons of fruits and vegetables are grown each year at The Land and are served in Walt Disney World restaurants.

40 Audio-Animatronics are in the Living with the Land attraction.

32,000 tomatoes and a total weight of 1,151.84 pounds have been harvested from one plant a Guinness world record.

Captain EO

1986 is when Captain EO debuted.

500 guests can view Captain EO.

17 minutes long, and costing $17 million, Captain EO set a record in the 1980s as minute-for-minute the most expensive Hollywood film.

Mission: SPACE

2003 is when Mission: Space debuted.

4 centrifuges, each with 10 cabins, are in the ride. Half (Orange Team) offer the original high speeds, while the other half (Green Team) offer the same ride, but the centrifuges don't engage, removing the high-speed effects.

40 guests is the vehicle capacity.

10 capsules are on each vehicle.

4 guests can fit into each capsule.

160 guests can ride simultaneously.

800 dollars a gallon is the cost of the special color-shifting paint used for Mission: SPACE.

40,000 square feet is the size of the attraction building.

6 minutes is all it will take to get you to Mars and back.

16 feet in diameter is Jupiter and is the biggest celestial body in the Planetary Plaza.

53,809,920 jellybeans would fill the Jupiter sphere.

10 feet in diameter is Earth sphere.

13,136,640 jellybeans would fill it.

12 feet in diameter is the moon sphere.

22,702,080 jellybeans would fill it.

650 Walt Disney Imagineers spent more than 350,000 hours (the equivalent of 40 years of time) to develop Mission: SPACE, over a 5-year period.

100 shades of red were mocked up before the Imagineers decided on the color of the red planet that dominates the dramatic exterior of the attraction building.

10 legendary quotes by famed space explorers and supporters of space exploration are located around the walls of Planetary Plaza.

45,000 square-feet building includes the ISTC (International Space Training Center) in the year 2036.

100 million dollars was the cost to build.

21 cast members work at Mission:SPACE, which is more than at any other attraction. On busy days 32 cast members work here.

35 feet is the height of Mission: SPACE.

1,500-square-foot merchandise location, including astronaut-inspired gear, is located here.

25 space experts from NASA and the Jet Propulsion Laboratory, including five astronauts, were consulted in the creation of this attraction.

1959 and 1976, the United States and the Soviet Union sent 29 missions to the moon. The landing sites of all those missions are indicated on the moon sphere in the Planetary Plaza, with a single red marker denoting where Apollo 11 landed on July 20, 1969..

1 ride system has more computing power than a space shuttle, and there are 4 ride systems at this attraction.

2 primary computers on-board the ride system control all ride and show functions. In addition, there are 30 motion-control computers on board that handle capsule altitude during the flight, and a show-control computer that operates the interactive functions within each capsule.

1 RPM and 35 feet tall, with a diameter of 32 feet, is the Gravity Wheel in the Space Simulation Lab.

The Seas with Nemo & Friends

2006 is when The Seas with Nemo & Friends.

15 minutes is the length of each show.

130 guests can see each show.

2,200 guest per hour can ride this attraction.

SeaBase

27 feet deep is the SeaBase tank.

5,700,000 gallons of water are used at the Sea Base and the Caribbean Coral Reef Aquarium.

203 feet is the diameter of the tank.

8,500 inhabitants live in SeaBase, consisting of over 100 different species of marine life. In order to keep all its residents comfortable, the temperature of the tank is closely monitored.

8' by 24', and 9,000 pounds, is the size and weight of each glass window pane.

6–8 inches thick is the glass on the observatory level.

1 inch of water siphoned off the top of the Living Seas tank would fill a regular-sized swimming pool. That's about 20,000 gallons.

400 pounds of food is fed to the sea animals each day.

2 tons of food is produced each week for the inhabitants of the Seas. Dolphins dine on herring and capelin; the West Indian manatees eat lettuce, carrots, sprouts, and fruit.

185,000 square feet were used for this attraction.

22 months were needed to construct it.

Turtle Talk with Crush

10 minutes of chat is all you get at Turtle Talk with Crush.

161 years old is the current age of Crush.

Soarin'

2005 is when Soarin' debuted.

4 minutes and 41 seconds is the ride time.

5-5-0-5 is the flight number that will be called; it's also the date the ride opened.

48 frames per second are projected to make the Soarin' movie.

3 scents are in Soarin': orange blossoms, pines, and ocean breeze.

2 theaters are housed in the Soarin' building.

3 lifters are used in each of the simulators.

37 tons can be lifted by the simulators.

3 rows are in each simulator.

59,895 square feet is the total space Soarin' occupies, including the ticketing area, Great Hall, skyway, Concourses 1 and 2, gate areas, and two flight theaters.

40 feet in the air is the highest point a guest will be lifted.

1 million pounds of steel provide the ride structure, and 37 tons are lifted during each ride cycle.

1,000 horsepower motors are needed to lift all the passengers for their flight.

80 feet in diameter projection screen dome is used for the movie.

87 guests can ride per each cycle of Soarin' in each theater.

11 locations are visited: San Francisco, Monterey Coast, Yosemite National Park, Napa Valley, Lake Tahoe, Palm Springs, San Diego, Anza-Borrego Desert State Park, Los Angeles, Malibu, and Disneyland.

14 aircraft can be seen in the movie: 9 balloons, 1 glider, 3 jets, and 1 helicopter.

Spaceship Earth

1982 is when Spaceship Earth debuted.

152 ride vehicles are used.

4 guests can ride in each vehicle.

2,400 guests can ride though Spaceship Earth each hour.

308 guests can ride at once.

14 minutes is the time of the ride.

185 feet tall is Spaceship Earth, making it visible from anywhere in Epcot.

5,181.1 feet is its circumference.

165 feet is its diameter.

18 stories tall is its height.

16 million pounds is its gross weight.

11,324 triangular panels made of aluminum alloy were used to build the geodesic sphere; each one is a custom fit.

57 historically accurate Audio-Animatronics are used in the attraction.

163 feet above the ground is how high your vehicle will travel.

6 legs hold up Spaceship Earth, each supported by pylons sunk 120–185 feet into the ground. At its lowest point, the slightly imperfect sphere stands 18 feet off the ground.

100 steel pilings are used to support the foundation and are 150 feet deep.

16 million pounds is the approximate weight of Spaceship Earth; it's more than three times that of a Space Shuttle fully fueled and ready for launch.

150,000 square feet, with an inside volume of 2,200,000 cubic feet, is the size of the sphere.

2.2 million cubic feet of space, with an outside surface diameter of 150,000 square feet, is encompassed in Spaceship Earth.

1 inch space between each triangle tile on Spaceship Earth allows for expansion and contraction in the Floridian climate.

80 powerful lighting fixtures illuminate Spaceship Earth each night.

109,375 square feet is the site area that was used for Spaceship Earth.

20 degrees is the average angle of descent of the track.

39 degrees is the steepest angle.

40,800 labor hours were needed to build Spaceship Earth.

1,700 tons of steel were used in its construction.

4 narrators have done the Spaceship Earth spiel in its history. The latest is actress Judi Dench.

Test Track

1999 is when Test Track debuted.

192 guests can ride per cycle.

6 guests can ride in each vehicle.

7 tests are performed on your car.

250 horsepower engines power the cars, which is more powerful than most cars on the road today.

50 degree banked turn is on Test Track.

3 on-board computers in each car (which have more processing power than the computers aboard the Space Shuttle) steer passengers through 5+ minutes of road tests.

5,246 feet is the total length of Test Track.

2,600 feet of the track are on the outside of the building.

6 different braking systems are on each car.

194 zones exist in the attraction, and a vehicle must read the tags (located under the track) as it travels throughout the course. If a vehicle misses reading 2 tags in a row, then the vehicle will cause a zone stop. If the ride computer loses track of a vehicle, this will also cause a zone stop.

2–16 and 18–33 are the number of the cars on Test Track; number 17 was destroyed during a worst-case scenario test before the ride opened.

50,000 miles will be driven on each car annually.

1 million miles is the estimated mileage each car was designed to last. That's 20 years!

34 turns are on Test Track from beginning to end.

22 wheels, only 4 of which are visible, are on each car.

65 mph is the top speed you can reach.

$100 million was the approximate cost to build Test Track.

200 mph is the wind force the track can withstand.

65 feet high and 320 feet in diameter is the size of the building which houses the ride, queue area, and post-show area.

8.8 seconds is required to go from 0–65 mph in the Test Track.

32 vehicles in total exist.

3 test vehicles can be loaded at one time.

25–26 vehicles can be used simultaneously.

720 times per day the crash-test dummies will be struck in the chest, banged on the knees, and have their necks bent in pre-show demonstrations.

50 degree bank is outside the building.

85 road signs line the Test Track road.

3 acres were used for this attraction.

24 feet is the maximum height from the ground that the track will reach.

100 degrees is the difference between the hot and cold rooms.

20 hours a day is how long the ride is left running due to the lengthy start time and nightly maintenance procedures.

World Showcase
....

11 pavilions make up the World Showcase.

9 pavilions were present on opening day 10/1/1982.

1 pavilion is hosted by the country it represents, and that is Morocco.

26 feet above the waterline are the 19 torches around the World Showcase.

26,000 feet is the length of the lights that outline the 11 pavilions; it's enough to stretch across the Golden Gate bridge more than 6 times.

30 pavilions is the number of pavilions originally planned to be in World Showcase. The original design was connected semi-circles dubbed "The Courtyard of Nations", and it was to include a observation tower that overlooked them all.

1.25 miles is the total length around World Showcase.

7 additional pavilions have been planned, but have never it made it past the drawing board, including Australia, Russia, Spain, Venezuela, United Arab Emirates, and Israel.

American Adventure

1982 is when the American Adventure debuted.

110,000 bricks make up the American Adventure building.

108,000 square feet is its size.

3 years of research went into its design and construction.

130' by 50' is the size of the stage.

28' by 155' is the size of the screen, which makes this the largest rear projection screen ever.

70mm film is used for the show.

65' by 35' scene-changer weighing 175 tons moves the show sets into place horizontally.

3 Benjamin Franklin figures are used.

3 Mark Twains figures are also used.

12 statues on the sides of the auditorium represent the Spirits of America.

44 flags are on display.

35 Audio-Animatronic figures are used in a variety of historical scenes such as Plymouth Rock, Valley Forge, and the Civil War. In fact, the Benjamin Franklin figure was one of the most sophisticated and detailed ever created. His groundbreaking ability to "walk" up stairs, coupled with the subtle twists of his body, and his hand-and-mouth movements, raised the bar in this technology.

2,048 guests can see the show each hour.

1,024 guests can be seated for each show.

28 minutes and 40 seconds is the length of show.

Canada Pavilion

1982 is when the Canada Pavilion debuted.

3 stories tall is the Hotel Du Canada, even though it looks 6 stories tall.

600 guests can fit in the Canada theater (no seats).

14 minutes is the length of the *O Canada!* film.

China Pavilion

1982 is when the China Pavilion debuted.

20 minutes is the length of the *Reflections of China* film.

200 guests can view the film at once (no seats).

1,000 servings of the General Tso dumplings are served every day in China.

500,000 General Tso dumplings are served each year in China.

2 films have been shown at the China Pavilion: *The Wonders of China* and *Reflections of China*.

France Pavilion

1982 is when the France Pavilion debuted.

103 feet above the France Pavilion raise the replica of the Eiffel Tower.

76 feet is the height of the Eiffel Tower at the France pavilion; the real Eiffel Tower is 1,063 feet in height.

18 minutes is the length of the *Impressions de France* film.

325 guest is the maximum capacity of the France theater.

German Pavilion

1982 is when the German Pavilion debuted.

26.2 miles of bratwurst are served every 60 days at the Biergarten restaurant. That's about 176 miles every year!

2,000 slices of apple strudel are served every day.

50 loaves of apple strudel are made each day.

2 pounds are dough are used to make 1 loaf of apple strudel.

3 hours of music can he heard on the Germany play loop before it repeats a song.

Italy Pavilion

1982 is when the Italy Pavilion debuted.

83-foot bell tower in the Italy Pavilion is an authentic replica of the original Campanile in St. Mark's Square in Italy.

2007 is when L'Originale Alfredo di Roma Ristorante, which had been open since 1982, was replaced by Via Napoli.

Japan Pavilion

1982 is when the Japan Pavilion debuted.

2003 is when Bijutsukan Gallery debuted.

83-foot-tall blue-roofed Gojunoto pagoda, the icon of the Japan Pavilion, is inspired by the seventh century Horyuji Shrine at Nara in Japan.

Norway Pavilion

1988 is when the Norway Pavilion debuted.

2014 is when the Maelstrom attraction was closed.

United Kingdom Pavilion

1982 is when the United Kingdom Pavilion debuted.

55 degrees is the temperature of the Guinness at the Rose & Crown Pub.

Mexico Pavilion

1982 is when the Mexico Pavilion debuted.

1982 is when Gran Fiesta Tour debuted.

250 guests can ride at once.

8 people per boat in 3 rows can ride.

8 minutes is the time of the Gran Fiesta Tour.

70 different tequilas are severed at the bar La Cava del Tequila.

30 seats are available there.

Innoventions Fountain

2,000 gallons of water would be used if all the water cannons in the fountain were fired at the same time.

304 nozzles and "shooters" can propel water over 150 feet in the air.

3 months of computer programming were needed to design the water ballets that run every 15 minutes.

1,068 colored lights focus on the streams of water at the fountain at night.

212 micro-shooters located in the upper pool each propel 2 gallons of water up to 80 feet.

40 mini-shooters located in the lower pool each propel 5 gallons of water up to 100 feet.

12 super-shooters located in the upper pool each propel 50 gallons of water up to 150 feet.

60 spray nozzle air accumulators for the super-shooters activate with pressures of 30–120 psi.

190,000 feet (35 miles) of electrical wire and 22,000 feet (4 miles) of conduit are used at the fountain.

23 countries brought water from 23 different rivers and lakes from around the world to dump into the fountain.

Epcot Parades & Shows

IllumiNations: Reflections of Earth

1988 is when IllumiNations debuted.

15 minutes is the time of the show.

2,800 fireworks are used.

750 mortar tubes are used.

56 firing modules are needed to shoot the fireworks.

34 firing positions are used around the lagoon.

1,000 computer-timed fireworks are in the show.

2,800 firework shells are used each night.

350,000 pounds is the gross weight of the globe in the show.

20 million ping-pong balls can be held in the globe.

15,000 LEDs are used on the outer shell of the globe, which is the world's first spherical video display system.

4 floating barges are also used to shoot fireworks.

4 fountain barges are used to create the water fountains.

40 feet is how high the fountains can shoot.

3-story video screens projecting vivid pictorial images that celebrate both human diversity and the unified spirit of human-kind come out of the globe.

300 images can be displayed on the globe.

6 computers are on the globe barge to run the globe.

67 computers operate IllumiNations.

40 locations around the lagoon house these computers.

30% more fireworks are used in this show than in any other previous show at Epcot.

350 tons is the weight of the globe barge.

180,000 light-emitting diodes are on the globe.

258 strobe lights are also there to add to the lighting effects.

1 year was needed to construct the globe.

175 tons is its gross weights.

2 days were needed to move the globe from its site to the Epcot lagoon.

4-ton crane moved the globe into position on the lagoon.

37 propane nozzles are used on the "inferno" barge.

0.5 miles of propane piping is used on this barge for the fire effects.

150,000 pounds is the weight of the inferno barge.

26,000 feet of lights outline the World Showcase pavilions; that is nearly 5 miles of lights.

1 pavilion does not participate in the show: Morocco.

Epcot International Flower and Garden Festival (2014)

30 million blooms blanket the park throughout the festival, which runs for 75 days.

11 outdoor kitchens feature sweet and savory food and beverage menu items. Each marketplace features a produce and herb garden to represent more than 50 overall beverage choices and more than 40 food items.

99 topiaries are placed throughout the park; 79 of them are character topiaries.

15 varieties of flowers, plants, and other garden materials are used to create the topiaries.

1/3 acre is the size of the Mike & Sulley's Monstrous Garden, a themed playground for children and one of the largest festival gardens created, with large, leafy plants including elephant ears, rubber plants, sea grapes, fiddle leaf fig, banana plants, and bromeliads and hibiscus.

4,300 pounds is the weight of Sulley topiary; it is one of Disney's largest. About 4,000 small plants fill his 13-foot frame.

2 new topiary stars are Kermit and Miss Piggy. Dozens of additional character topiaries represent Timon and Pumbaa, Cinderella, Belle and Beast, and Phineas and Ferb.

25 different plants, grasses, and mosses of various colors, including pink and red begonias, dusty miller, palm fiber, palm seeds, ficus, and lichen, are used to create and define facial and other features of character topiaries.

1,000 native butterflies represent up to 10 species at Tinker Bell's Butterfly House. Among the garden's two dozen nectar plants are Cape Royal plumbago, passion flower, coral honeysuckle, blazing star, butterfly bush, scarlet milkweed, and canna lily.

500,000 plants, trees, and shrubs are planted for the festival; 250,000 of those are annual blossoms.

60 different species of trees, 47 types of palms, and 48 varieties of bedding plants are used.

150 hands-on gardening demonstrations and seminars are presented.

30 "flower towers" of several varieties of blooms and plants line Innoventions Plaza.

225 floating mini-gardens, each three feet in diameter, of multi-hued impatiens provide splashes of color on two ponds that border the walkway between Future World and World Showcase.

700 container gardens of flowers, herbs, plants, and vegetables in clay pots, barrels, and urns enhance the landscape.

400 Walt Disney World horticulturists are needed to install the festival landscape, topiaries, and exhibits.

100 Epcot horticulturists maintain topiaries and other festival displays.

1 full year and about 24,000 cast member hours are needed to prepare for each annual festival.

Epcot International Food & Wine Festival (2013)

300 national and international wines are featured at the festival.

46 days long, the Food & Wine Festival began in 1996 with a run of 30 days.

220 menu items are available, each priced at $3–$8.

100-plus celebrity chefs and 160 Walt Disney World chefs are involved.

300 wine and beer seminars take place during the festival.

138 Eat to the Beat! concerts are performed.

910,000 cranberries (over 3,000 pounds) will be used during the festival.

300,000 wine servings will be dispensed; if laid end-to-end, the number of wine glasses used would reach from Walt Disney World to the Disney Cruise Line terminal at Port Canaveral.

360,000 beer servings will be dispenses, enough to fill the aquariums 5 times over at Rainforest Café at Disney's Animal Kingdom.

100,000 dessert servings will be tasted at the "3D" Disney's Dessert Discovery parties.

Epcot Extinct Attractions

Honey, I Shrunk the Audience

1994 is when Honey, I Shrunk the Audience debuted.

570 guests can sit in the theater.

13 minutes was the time of the show.

Horizons

1983 is when Horizons debuted.

1994 is when Horizons became seasonal.

1999 is when Horizons was retired.

2000 is when Horizons was demolished.

174 vehicles were used.

2,784 guests could ride per hour.

15 minutes was the time of the show.

1,346 was the track length.

$60,000,000.00 was the construction costs of Horizons.

136,835 was the square footage of the building.

37,000 was the square footage of the land.

17 show sets were used at Horizons.

7 murals were used.

54 Audio-Animatronic figures were used.

35 animated props were used.

110 lighting effects were used.

583 static props were used.

456 foliage plants were used.

14 film proctors were used.

36 screens were needed for all the proctors used.

Wonders of Life

76-foot-tall tower in front of Wonders of Life represents the double helix structure of DNA.

$100,000,000 was the cost of building Wonders of Life back in October 19, 1989.

5 billion times the size of actual human DNA is the tower outside the Wonders of Life.

100,000 square is the size of the show building.

25 tons would be the weight of the Double Helix.

250 feet wide is the size of the pavilions golden geodesic dome, making it 40% wider than Spaceship Earth.

2007 was the last year the pavilion operated.

26 tons is the weight of the simulators used in Body Wars.

Living Seas

1996 is when the Living Seas debuted.

2005 is when the Living Seas was retired.

7 minutes was the time of the show.

414 was the maximum guest capacity.

4 hydrolators were used as the ride vehicles.

5.7 million gallons of water fill the tank at the Living Seas. The aquarium is 200 feet in diameter, which is larger than Spaceship Earth.

Maelstrom

1988 is when Maelstrom debuted.

2014 is when Maelstrom closed.

16 people could ride on each Viking ship.

192 guests could ride at once.

1,920 guests could ride per hour.

964 was the track length.

Disney's Hollywood Studios

1989 is when Disney's MGM-Studio opened.

2007 is when the park's name changed to Disney's Hollywood Studio.

77 acres were used for the Hollywood Studio parking lot.

7,500 parking spaces available.

154 acres was used for the park.

$500 million is the estimated construction cost.

5 attractions and one exhibit were available on opening day: Monster Sound Show, SoundWorks (exhibit), SuperStar Television, the Great Movie Ride, Backstage Studio Tour, and the Magic of Disney Animation.

231 acres, including 77 acres of parking, encompass Disney's Hollywood Studios.

3 animation films were produced entirely in Florida: *Mulan*, *Lilo and Stitch*, and *Brother Bear*.

63,000 Cobb salads are tossed each year at the Hollywood Brown Derby. The original recipe for the dressing was created in 1926.

190 orders of meatloaf and mashed potatoes are served each day at the 50s Prime Time Café.

300,000 gallons of water are needed to fill the water tower.

0 gallons of water are in the water tower; its just a prop.

$335,433,448.00 is the taxable value of the park.

$77,851,018.00 is its land value.

$222,722,357.00 is the building value.

$4,699,503.11 is the amount of taxes paid in 2006.

35 feet into the air is the stainless steel ABC Commissary restaurant sign.

10-foot palm is in the entrance way of the ABC Commissary.

½ day experience was the original plan for this park during the concept stage.

Streets of America

"Honey, I Shrunk the Kids"
Movie Set Adventure

30 feet tall is one blade of grass in this play area and there are 47 of these blades in total.

16-foot-tall building block is here.

52-foot long garden hose is also here.

500 pounds of structural steel is used to support the blades of grass, which can withstand 80 mph winds. Each was wind-tested at Cal Tech prior to installation.

117 gigantic leaves are here.

3 stories tall are the mushroom caps.

45 blades of grass exist in the play area of Honey I shrunk The Kids exactly.

3 stories tall are the mushroom caps at the Movie Set Adventure.

Lights, Motors, Action! Extreme Stunt Show

5/5/2005 is opening day for Lights, Motors, Action! Extreme Stunt Show.

5,000 seats are in the stadium and 3,000 more can stand.

3 shows a day are performed.

30 minutes is the time of each show.

6.5 acres area is used to house stadium.

45–65 foot fireball is created for the show.

150 hp motorcycle engine are installed in each car.

4 forward gears and 4 reverse gears are used in each car.

1,300 lbs is the weight of each car, which is half that of a normal production vehicle.

40-vehicles used in the stunt show were gutted to reduce their weight and motorcycle engines installed so the cars can accelerate faster.

1,322 is the exact weight of each car.

177,000-square-foot facility is the size of the arena.

35 stunt drivers, actors, and technicians are used in each show.

20 custom-built cars, 10 stunt motorcycles, and two high-powered personal water crafts are available for the show.

3 hero cars are used in each show.

5 pursuit cars are used.

4 motorcycles are used.

2 personal watercraft are used.

10–12 crew members maintain the vehicles on site and ensure their safety before each show.

14 stunt drivers are needed for each show.

1 practice course is maintained backstage at Disney's Hollywood Studios. (The Epcot parking lot used to be the practice area until a permanent course was established.)

10 weeks of training is required for each driver before they ever get into a car to drive in a show.

Muppet Vision 3-D

1991 is when Jim Henson's Muppet Vision 3-D debuted.

584 guests can be seated in the theater.

25 minutes is the time of the show.

12 minute pre-show can be seen in the lobby.

3 rats can be found in the fountain outside the theater.

10 Audio-Animatronics are used.

Great Movie Ride

1989 is the year The Great Movie Ride debuted.

10 trams are used, but there are 12 available.

70 guests can ride in each tram.

560 guests can ride through the attraction each hour.

021429 is on the license plate of a gangster car in Gangster Alley. It's the date of the St. Valentine's Day massacre in Chicago, which took place on February 14, 1929.

22-foot central roof of Grauman's Chinese Theater section was constructed separately and hoisted into place by crane.

22 minutes is the time of your ride through the great movies.

59 Audio-Animatronic figures are in the ride, including Gene Kelly, Julie Andrews, Dick Van Dyke, James Cagney, John Wayne, Clint Eastwood, Sigourney Weaver, Humphrey Bogart, Ingrid Bergman, and Margaret Hamilton (the Wicked Witch of the West).

12 films are depicted: *Footlight Parade, Singin' in the Rain, Mary Poppins, The Public Enemy, The Searchers, Pale Rider, Alien, Raiders of the Lost Ark, Tarzan and His Mate, Casablanca, Fantasia,* and *The Wizard of Oz.*

1933 is the year of the oldest movie depicted (Footlight Parade).

95,000 square feet are taken up by this attraction.

1,928 feet is the length of the ride track.

3,000 effects are used.

3 *Wizard of Oz* scenes were built for the Great Movie Ride.

Indiana Jones Epic Stunt Spectacular

1989 is when Indiana Jones Epic Stunt Spectacular debuted.

2,000 guests can sit in the amphitheater.

35 minutes is the length of the show.

8/25/1989 was the date of the first show.

12 foot diameter boulder is used during the show.

400 is the pretend weight of the boulder.

100 tons is the approximate weight of the moving sets, making them the largest moving sets in history.

17 stunt performers are conduct all the stunts.

Pixar Place

Toy Story Mania

2008 is when Toy Story Mania debuted.

4 guests can seat in each ride vehicle.

108 guests can ride at once.

30 seconds of play is allowed for each section of the ride.

5 minutes is the total ride time.

8,500 Woody dolls weigh the same as 1 ride vehicle.

5,026 toy soldiers would have to line up end-to-end to equal the track length.

1 million virtual plates are broken each day.

6 mini-games are available.

$80 million was the estimated cost to design and build Toy Story Mania.

3 components make up the ride control system: 1 for the ride vehicles, 1 for the games, and 1 for the special effects.

150 computers are used, including 1 HP Windows XP PC for each of the game screens.

56 game screens are used.

2 tracking systems provide the game control system with the vehicle's exact location, making sure that gameplay is not affected by even minor differences in vehicle position.

3 sub-systems work together to handle any show control contingency that may occur.

1st attraction that Walt Disney Imagineering designed where the Imagineers had to wear 3-D glasses to art direct all the black-light paint elements.

4 feet is the diameter of the viewfinder at Toy Story Mania.

13 inches long is the length of the Christmas bulbs in the queue.

5'6" person will feel about 14" tall in Andy's room.

$6 in change can be seen falling out of Hamm in the final scene.

Mickey Avenue

Walt Disney: One Man's Dream

2001 is when Walt Disney: One Man's Dream debuted.

200 guests can be seated in the theater.

16 minutes is the length of the film presenting Walt Disney's life.

Animation Courtyard

The Magic of Disney Animation

1989 is when The Magic of Disney Animation debuted.

50 guests can be seated here.

Playhouse Disney—Live on Stage

2001 is when Playhouse Disney—Live on Stage debuted.

10 shows per day are performed.

20 minutes is the length of the show

600 guests can sit in the theater.

Voyage of the Little Mermaid

1992 is when Voyage of the Little Mermaid debuted.

12 feet tall and 10 feet wide is the size of the Ursula puppet.

17 minutes is the time of the show.

600 guests can watch the show at once.

100 puppets are in the show.

Sunset Boulevard

Fantasmic!

1998 is when Fantasmic! debuted.

25 minutes is the time of the show.

6,900 guests can be seated in the theater.

3,000 guests can stand in the theater.

$20,000 per show is the estimated cost of presentation.

32,000 pounds is what Maleficent in her dragon form weighs, with a 50 foot wingspan. She also rises 50 feet into the air.

1.9 million gallons of water are in the moat that surrounds the stage.

800 gallons of water per minute are used for the 3 mist screens.

46 performers are used in each show.

57.5 feet above the water stands the mountain.

80 feet is the length of the steamboat; it weights 70,000 pounds.

350 lights are used.

78 costumes are used.

26 Disney characters are in the finale.

Beauty and the Beast—Live on Stage

1991 is when Beauty and the Beast—Live on Stage debuted.

20 minutes is the time of the show.

1,500 guests can be seated in the theater.

8 feet is the wingspan of the bats used in the show.

Rock 'n' Roller Coaster

1999 is when Rock 'n' Roller Coaster debuted.

24 guests can ride in each limo.

1.22 minutes is the total ride time.

3.12 minutes is the cycle time of each ride, which is the exact running time of one of Aerosmith's biggest hits, "Sweet Emotion".

2 minutes is the attraction's pre-show length.

900 speakers are in the ride.

5 speakers are located in each seat.

3,403 feet of track is used, which is more than a half-mile of twists, turns, loops, corkscrews, hills, and dips.

5 license plates are on the Aerosmith limos: QKLIMO, UGOGIRL, BUHBYE, 2FAST4U, H8TRFFC.

3 inversions, 2 rollover loops and 1 corkscrew: these were all firsts for a Disney World ride.

40 feet tall is the giant guitar icon.

0–60 in 2.8 seconds is how fast the coaster travels.

3 different soundtracks are used, each one specific to the limo on which it is played.

200 feet of track are used in the launch to create the 4 and 5 "G" forces.

120 speakers and 24 sub-woofers are in each limo.

32,000 watts can be produced by the onboard sound system of each limo.

1 mile of neon light is used outside the attraction.

3,536 marbles adorn the 2 doors you see as your enter the queue area.

15 times its normal size is the Fender Stratocaster that sits outside the show building.

40 feet tall is its height.

32 feet is the length of the Stratocaster's neck.

80 feet is the highest point of the track.

3.7 million cubic foot is the size of the show building.

37 million cubic feet of space are located inside the building.

1,500 guest can ride per hour.

5 limos can operate at the same time.

1 new electrical substation was built to supply power to this attraction.

12 times is how often Steven Tyler and Joe Perry rode the attraction when they came to Disney World for the first time.

80 Chevrolet Corvettes were used to make a giant Fender Stratocaster in the parking lot to celebrate the ride's 1-year anniversary. All the cars were red, black, and white.

The Twilight Zone Tower of Terror

1994 is when The Twilight Zone Tower of Terror debuted.

6 elevators shafts are in the attraction.

8 elevator cars can be run simultaneously.

21 guests can ride in each elevator.

4 minutes is the time of the ride.

1996 is when version 2 ("Twice the Fright") made its appearance and added a second drop to the ride.

1999 is when version 3 ("Fear in Every Drop") made the drop sequence more complex with a series of false starts and sudden stops before finally falling to the basement.

2002 is when version 4 ("Never the Same Fear Twice") put the computers in control so that each drop involved a different randomly selected sequence of events.

4 loading zones are used and merge into 2 paths on the top floor.

2 years were needed to reprogram the Tower of Terror computers to the new T4 configuration.

7 feet wide, 35 feet long, and 133,000 pounds is the size of 1 motor.

15 times the speed of a normal elevator is the rate at which these motors can push the cars.

275 Corvettes are needed to produce the same amount of torque as the Tower of Terror motors.

1.5 seconds is all it takes to reach top speed in the finale and then come to a complete stop, all in 130 feet.

10259 is the number on the "inspection certificate" for the elevators. It's the date (10/02/1959) that Rod Serling's influential TV show premiered.

13 stories is the total plummet.

199 feet tall is the height of the tower, which was struck by lightning during construction.

1 extra foot over 199 feet and this attraction would require a red blinking light on top as required by the FAA.

13-diamond rating plaque hangs in the lobby from the American Automobile Association. Their real ratings only go to up to 5 diamonds.

1939 is when the real Hollywood Tower Hotel was struck by lightning.

1997 is when the Disney version of the hotel was actually struck by lightning.

12 is the number of floors listed on the elevator dial.

1959 is the last time the elevator was inspected and also the first year that the *Twilight Zone* aired on television.

156 is the total number of episodes of the original *Twilight Zone* television show.

2 is the number of time the Imagineers watched each and every one of those episodes as part of their research.

5 guests were in the elevator at the Hollywood Tower Hotel when it was struck by lighting, according to the pre-show.

1,000 dollars is the cost of each cast member costume, making them the most expensive costumes on property.

110,000 pounds of torque are generated by each of the 2 ride engines.

132,000 pounds is the weight of the ride engines.

35 feet long is their length.

7 feet tall is their height.

1,500 tons of steel and 145,800 cubic feet of concrete were used in the construction of the Tower of Terror.

27,000 roof tiles were used.

20 different songs are played in the lobby.

Extinct Attractions, Shows, and Parades
....

Sorcerer Mickey Hat

122 feet is the height of the Sorcerer Mickey Hat, which means that Mickey Mouse would have to be 350 feet tall, and wear a hat size of 605 7/8, if he were to put it on.

156-ton hat was created in honor of the 100th birthday celebration for Walt Disney.

27 tons is the weight of just the brim and cone of the hat.

1 football field's worth of concrete was used to cover the hat at a 1-foot depth.

60,000 cubic feet is the interior size of the hat; upside-down, it could hold 444,744 gallons of water.

13,493 bolts hold the hat together.

26,986 washers were used in the construction of the hat.

17,000 feet of underground utility piping keep the hat together.

6 stars are on the hat.

2 moons are on it, too.

500 Cadillac's worth of paint were needed to cover the hat.

Block Party Bash

2008 is when the Block Party Bash Debuted.

1 show is performed daily.

15 minutes at each stop location is how long each float parties there.

114 cast members are in the parade.

30 crew members help with the parade.

Backlot Tour

1989 is when the Backlot Tour debuted.

200 guests can ride the back lot shuttle at one time.

25 minutes is the time of the ride.

70,000 gallons of water are used to re-create the flash flood in Catastrophe Canyon.

3.5 minutes is how it takes for the 70,000 gallons of water to be dumped each time.

4 tanks are used to release the water.

1,000 gallons of water is dumped on the person in the pilot house.

1,000 guests can be on the Backlot tour at once.

Sounds Dangerous with Drew Carey

1999 is when Sounds Dangerous with Drew Carey debuted.

12 minutes is the time of the show.

American Idol Experience

2009 is when the American Idol Experience debuted.

1100 guests can be seated in the theater.

35 x 7.5 foot screen makes this the largest curved screen on property.

113 video screens are used.

105 audio speakers are used.

735 lighting fixtures are used.

100 feet is the width of the stage.

3000 square feet is the size of the stage.

2000 votes can be tabulated in 2 seconds by the computers.

7 pm is the final show each day.

45 minutes is the length of the finale show.

76 miles of cable was used in constructing the attraction.

25 miles of conduit was used.

25,000 square feet of indoor space is available.

16 weeks were needed to build the set.

50 carpenters were used to build it.

4 audition rooms are where contestants try-out for the show.

1 producers room is where the decision is made as to who will be in the show that day.

3 performers are chosen for each of the 7 preliminary performances held each day, leading up to the evening finale featuring the top vote recipients of each of those 7 shows.

100 different song choices are available for the performers to select from, each with a unique lighting and background media package to give each singer the full American Idol treatment.

Journey Into Narnia: Prince Caspian

2008 is when Journey into Narnia debuted.

80 guests can fit into the pre-show area.

5 minutes is the time of the pre-show.

High School Musical 3: Right Here! Right Now!

2007 is when High School Musical 3: Right Here! Right Now! debuted.

6 shows are conducted each day.

14 performers are in the show.

20 minutes is the time of the show.

Disney's Animal Kingdom

1998 is when the Animal Kingdom opened.

403 acres were used for the park, making it the biggest park (in size) at Disney World.

8 years of planning and construction were needed to make the park.

3 years of construction were needed.

2,600 construction workers were employed.

$800 million dollars was spent.

60 dump trucks full of dirt were delivered to the construction site every day for 2 years straight to create the park's landscape.

4.4 million cubic yards of dirt were used.

60 miles of plumbing were laid.

1 million square feet of rock work were used during construction.

6,000 cars can park at the Animal Kingdom.

4,500 cast members work there.

8,000 tons of manure is the 4th largest recycled commodity of the Disney Company.

90-ton tree replanted in Harambe Village is the largest tree replanted.

4 million plants were put into the ground.

1,500 animals representing 300 species are at the park, most acquired from zoos accredited by the American Zoo and Aquarium Association.

5,000 specimens of fish representing 50 different species are at the park.

2,000 specimens of insects representing 40 different species are at the park.

4.5 tons of food is fed to the animals a day.

2,000 pounds of vegetation is fed to the animals every day.

40,000 worms are fed to the animals each week, including super mealworms, yellow mealworms, red wigglers, night crawlers, and wax worms.

$1.7 million dollars per year are spent on these worms.

80,000 crickets are consumed by the animals each month.

400 individual or group meals are prepared by the Animal Nutrition Center each day.

2.6 million gallons of water cycles though the park's treated-water system 5 times a day.

150 different animal species have been bred by the park.

4 million trees, plants, shrubs, ground-covers, vines, epiphytes, and grasses from every continent on Earth—except Antarctica—were planted at the Animal Kingdom.

40 types of palm trees are there.

260 grasses are there.

2,000 kinds of shrubs are there.

20 types of magnolia are there.

3,000 palm-like cycad are located in DinoLand USA.

600 wellness checks are conducted per year by the Animal Programs team.

40,000 samples of animal poop have been analyzed by the lab technicians since the park opened.

The Oasis

1998 is when the Oasis debuted.

1200 feet of trails are located here.

13 viewing areas are available from which to see the plants and animals.

Discovery Island

Tree of Life

1998 is when the Tree of Life debuted.

12 Imagineers created it.

13 artists worked on it.

1,500 hand-painted wooden animal carvings (each less than 3-feet long) can be found throughout Safari Village. Native craftsmen on the island of Bali carved the animals.

12 main branches are on the tree.

5 shades of green were used to color the leaves.

45 secondary limbs are on the tree.

8,692 branches are on the Tree of Life, from the largest to the smallest twig.

103,000 leaves were placed on the tree by hand.

19.4 is the number of miles the leaves would stretch if laid end to end.

145 feet high, the tree stretches over 165 feet at the widest point and has a trunk 50 feet in diameter.

145 is also the wind speed that the tree of life can withstand.

50 feet is the width of the tree at the middle.

170 feet is the width of the tree at the base.

324 images are on the Tree of Life. Jane Goodall, founder of the Jane Goodall Institute, was invited by Disney to visit the Animal Kingdom. She was very impressed, but noted that there were no chimpanzees on the tree. Imagineers went to work and not only added a chimp, they added Goodall's favorite, David Graybeard.

1 is the average number of animals an artist could carve in a day.

Discovery Island Trails
1998 is when Discovery Island Trails debuted.

27 million gallons of water are in Discovery River, enough to fill 1,800 average-sized backyard swimming pools.

It's Tough to Be a Bug!
1999 is when It's Tough to Be a Bug debuted.

450 guests can be seated in the theater.

8 minutes is the time of the show.

40 fans are used for special effects.

50 different experimental odors were tested before the smell of the stink bug was approved.

70,000 "perfume" pellets are needed for the stink bug effect.

74 functions are built into Hopper, making him one of the most complex Audio-Animatronics.

2 technicians work 8 hours each night on Hopper to keep him operating properly.

1999 is the year when It's Tough to Be a Bug won the Outstanding Attraction award from the Themed Entertainment Association.

Africa

1998 is when Africa debuted.

7 thatch huts are located in Africa.

15 semi-trailer trucks of Berg grass was used to create these huts.

13 Zulu craftsmen from Kwazulu-Natal, South Africa, were brought in to make the thatched roofs.

1,500 2–3 feet long fanciful hand-painted wooden folk art animal carvings (a fusion of pre-Columbian, Peruvian, African, and Polynesian forms) were crafted on the island of Bali by native craftsmen and can be seen adorning the architecture of Safari Village.

Kilimanjaro Safaris

1998 is when Kilimanjaro Safaris debuted.

110 acres in size makes Kilimanjaro Safaris the largest single attraction ever created by Disney, in fact, the entire Magic Kingdom can fit inside this one attraction.

250 African animals can be seen during the safari.

30-foot elevation was created for the African savannah, and over 50 acres were used.

18-foot deep and 21-foot wide moat separates the animal areas.

44 ride vehicles are available.

41 vehicles are on the route at any one time. They are kept separate by a sophisticated computer and "pucks" buried in the road.

32 guests fit in each vehicle.

2 miles is the length of the safari.

22 minutes is the total time of the safari.

1,344 guests can ride per hour.

12–18 months was the time the landscape was planted before the animals were released in their habitats.

Pangani Forest Exploration Trail

1998 is when Pangani Forest Exploration Trail debuted.

2055 feet is the length of the trail.

9 viewing area are on the trail.

28 species are on exhibit.

Festival of the Lion King

1998 is when Festival of the Lion King debuted.

7 shows are performed each day.

1,375 guests can be accommodated in the show theater.

28 minutes is the time of the show.

50 cast members perform in the show.

4 sections are in theater: elephant, giraffe, warthog, and lion.

12-foot tall Simba is animated and sits on top of Pride Rock.

1990 is when these floats were last used in Disney's California Adventure parade.

136 African-inspired costumes are used in the Festival of the Lion King.

Asia

1998 is when parts of Asia debuted.

120 artists worked more than 5 months to create the 4 murals that honor the former rulers of the mystical land of Anandapur.

Expedition Everest

2006 is when Expedition Everest debuted.

5 trains (or "steam donkeys") can run simultaneously, but only 4 typically run on a regular basis.

34 passengers can sit in each train.

6 cars are on every set of trains.

3 minutes is the total ride time.

1 mile of track is used on Expedition Everest.

6.4 acres of land were used.

3 years of construction were needed to create the "Mount Everest", the largest mountain at Disney World.

200 feet tall is the mountain, one of 18 mountains created by Disney Imagineers.

80 feet is the height of the drop.

1,800 tons of steel was used to create the mountain structure. That is 6 times the amount needed to create an office building of the same size.

5,000 tons of steel were used for the structure and track.

18.7 million pounds of concrete were used.

2,000 gallons of stain and paint were used.

218,000 square feet of rock were used.

260,000 pounds of thrust force are built into the Yeti, more then a 747 airplane.

8,000 authentic props were imported from Asia and are on display in the queue.

2,000 of these props were hand-crafted from wood, stone, and metal.

1+ acre of concrete 23-feet thick was needed to build the mountain.

5 acres of themed rock was carved to make it come to life.

900 Bamboo plants were used to create the lowlands near Mount Everest.

10 species of trees were planted there.

110 species of scrubs were planted there, too.

$100 million is the construction cost of Expedition Everest.

50 mph is how fast you travel on the coaster.

3,000 pre-fabricated "chips" created from 25,000 individually computer-molded pieces of steel were used to craft the mountain.

2,000 gallons of stain and paint were used on the rockwork and throughout the village. The color scheme has ritual meaning in the Himalayan culture.

32,000 bags of concrete were used to create the rockwork.

320 feet above sea level would make Mount Everest the fourth highest point in Florida if it were a real mountain.

19 different functions are built into the Yeti.

5 feet is how far the Yeti can move in and out on the boom that is attached to his back.

18 inches is how much the Yeti can move up and down.

20 seconds is the total time needed to recharge the Yeti hydraulic system.

6,000 pounds of fur were used to make the Yeti's outer coat.

1,000 square feet of fur were used for his outer skin.

1,000 snaps are used to keep the fur attached.

250 zippers are also used.

24 models were created of Expedition Everest before the final design was approved.

6 inches is all that separates the track from the structure of the mountain.

Kali River Rapids

1999 is when Kali River Rapids debuted.

25 feet is the height of the drop.

7 pumps are used to pump all the water for this attraction.

26,000 gallons of water are pumped each minute by these pumps.

12 rafts are used.

12–20 guests can ride in each raft.

4 minutes and 30 seconds is the time of the ride.

2800 guests can ride Kali River Rapids each hour.

5000 props were used.

90 feet is the height of the incline at the start of the ride.

1st attraction ever to have the feature FastPass tickets was Kali River Rapids.

Maharaji Jungle Trek

1998 is when Maharaji Jungle Trek debuted.

7 viewing area are available.

6 tigers are here.

18–20 hours a day the tigers at the Maharajah Jungle Trek are sleeping.

70 degrees is the temperature of the tiger pool (which has fish for the tigers to eat).

Flights of Wonder

1998 is the year when Flights of Wonder debuted.

25 minutes is the time of the show.

1,150 guests can sit in the show theater.

Rafiki's Planet Watch
....

1998 is when Rafiki's Planet Watch debuted.

Conservation Station

1998 is when Conservation Station debuted.

49 species are on exhibit here.

Wildlife Express

1.2 miles is the length of the Wildlife Express train route.

10 miles per hour is the top speed of the train.

50 guests can be seated in each car.

5 trains are operational.

2.2 feet wide is the width of the Wildlife Express track.

2-4-2 is the wheel configuration of the locomotives.

1997 was the year the trains were built.

DinoLand U.S.A.
....

1998 is when DinoLand U.S.A. debuted.

450 pounds is the weight of Lucky, the first free-roaming Audio-Animatronic.

9 feet tall and 12 feet long is his size.

The Boneyard

1998 is when the Boneyard debuted.

500 guests is its maximum capacity.

DINOSAUR

1998 is when DINOSAUR debuted as Countdown to Extinction.

12 passengers fit in each all-terrain vehicle.

144 guests can ride Dinosaur at once.

19 dinosaurs can be seen on the ride, which uses a system modeled after the Indiana Jones and the Temple of the Forbidden Eye attraction at Disneyland.

100 gallon tank of hydraulic fluid is used for the dinosaurs.

3 minutes, 30 seconds is the total ride time.

3,000 psi is needed to move most of the dinosaurs; that is more than what is needed at any other Disney World attractions.

11 Audio-Animatronics are in DINOSAUR.

40-foot-tall brachiosaurus greets you at the entrance.

Primeval Whirl

2002 is when Primeval Whirl debuted.

2 minutes, 30 seconds is the ride time.

4 guests can ride in each vehicle.

52 guests can ride at once on each of the 2 tracks.

13 colorful ride vehicles are available that whirl past flying asteroids and corny depictions of dinosaur cutouts that spin and pop up along the track.

TriceraTop Spin

2002 is when TriceraTop Spin debuted.

2 minutes is the ride time.

16 ride vehicles are available.

4 guests can ride in each one.

64 guests can ride at once.

Finding Nemo—The Musical

2007 is when Finding Nemo—The Musical debuted.

35 minutes is the time of the show.

1,500 guests can fit into the theatre per show.

4 shows are performed daily.

18 musical theater actors and dancers perform.

6,000 square foot show deck is used, which is larger then 3 Broadway shows.

40 puppets are used.

12 inches long is the smallest puppet, Blenny.

19 feet tall is the largest puppet, Nigel.

2 puppeteers are needed to operate Nigel.

Animal Kingdom Extinct Attractions, Shows and Parades

Camp Minnie-Mickey Greeting Trails

1998 is when Camp Minnie-Mickey Greeting Trails debuted.

Pocahontas and Her Forest Friends

1998 is when Pocahontas and Her Forest Friends debuted.

8 shows are performed each day.

350 people can be seated in the tree-shaded theater at once.

15 minutes is the time of the show.

Mickey's Jammin' Jungle Parade

2001 is when Mickey's Jammin Jungle Parade debuted.

15 minutes is the approximate time of the parade.

5 character-based safari vehicles are used.

4 drum sculptures are used.

3 rickshaw taxis are used.

8 animal puppets are used.

16 Disney characters are used.

10 party animal stilt walkers are used.

10 party patrols are used.

8 abstract animal puppets were designed by Michael Curry Designs in Portland, Oregon, which also created the puppets for *The Lion King* on Broadway.

60 cast members, including performers, drivers, and coordinators, participate in the parade.

25 spectators will be selected daily to ride in the opening unit, 3 guest rickshaws, and the finale unit. Guests will be given Kodak disposable cameras so they can capture their special moment.

Walt Disney World Water Parks

Typhoon Lagoon

1989 is when Typhon Lagoon debuted.

56 acres was used for the park.

2.75 million gallons of water are used in the wave pool.

2,100 foot "lazy river" is called Castaway Creek.

15 feet is the creek width.

3 feet is its depth.

2 feet per second is how fast the current moves.

95 foot tall Mt. Mayday is surrounded by a 2.75-million-gallon wave pool.

2 times the size of football filed is the size of the inland surfing lagoon.

6½ feet tall are the waves generated by the wave machine

19.5 acres is the size of the guest parking lot.

1,000 parking spaces for guest are located there.

1350 gallons of water per minute is pumped from the Crush "n" Gusher water jets.

362,000 gallon saltwater pool is the shark reef.

2.5 acre wave-making lagoon pool is in the park.

80,000 gallons of water are used in the surf pool.

18 activity spots are in the Ketchakiddee Creek play area.

90 seconds is how often waves are created in the surf pool.

214 feet is the length of Humunga Kowabunga slide.

3 tubes can be used on it.

60-degree angle is on the slide.

30 mph is your maximum speed on Humunga Kowabunga.

35 feet is the height of the Bay Slides.

400-foot slide called Keelhaul Falls is in the park.

460-foot long slide called Mayday Falls is here, too.

300 feet is the length of Gangplank Falls.

1 slide from Crush 'n' Gusher can fill a standard home-size pool in about 1 minute.

3 hours would be needed for Crush 'n' Gusher to fill up the wave pool with 2.7 million gallons of water.

Blizzard Beach

1996 is when Blizzard Beach debuted.

1-acre wave pool is called Meltaway Bay.

3,000-foot slow-moving Cross Country Creek, the "lazy river" that flows around the perimeter of the park.

2.5 feet is the depth of this river.

120-foot high Mount Gushmore is the 5th highest point in Florida.

3 colored slopes are at Mount Gushmore to aid guests navigating around the park: green, red and purple.

66 acres make Blizzard beach the larger of the 2 Disney World water parks.

21 slides, 1 massive wave pool, and separate areas for pre-teens and young children are here.

120 feet tall is Summit Plummet, the 2nd tallest free-fall slide.

1,400 feet makes Teamboat Springs the world's longest "family white-water raft ride".

4–6 people can ride per raft at Teamboat Springs.

90-feet tall is Slush Gusher.

250 feet is its length.

35 mph is the top speed you can reach on Slush Gusher.

50 feet high is Downhill Double Dipper.

230 feet is its length.

25 mph is the top speed on Downhill Double Dipper.

350 feet long is Snow Stormers.

8 lanes of racing can be found at Toboggan Racers.

250 feet long is its length.

127 steps must be climbed to reach the top of Runoff Rapids.

3 flumes are there.

2 guests can ride in 1 tube.

600 feet is the length of Runoff Rapids.

66 degree is the tilt on Summit Plummet.

350 feet is the height of the flume there.

55 mph is the top speed you can reach on Summit Plummet.

$42,583,611.00 is the taxable value of Blizzard Beach.

$21,306,265.00 is the building value.

$596,606.61 is the amount of taxes paid in 2006.

Walt Disney World Resorts

Grand Floridian Resort & Spa

54 acres make up this resort with a turn-of-the-century Victorian theme.

8 buildings encompass the Grand Floridian and 3 other building are used for the spa, Narcoosee's restaurant, and the convention center.

867 rooms and suites are available.

2 pools are at the resort.

40,000 square feet of convention space are there.

1 ballroom can also be found in the convention space as well as 16 breakout rooms.

$121,588,561.00 id the taxable value of the resort.

$33,379,500.00 is the land value.

$88,209,061.00 is the building value.

$1,703,484.92 is the amount of taxes paid in 2006.

440 square feet is the size of the room with 2 queen beds.

5 stories tall is the height of the atrium.

3 stain glass domes can be found in the ceiling of the atrium.

4 detached buildings contain most of the rooms.

181-foot slide is at the beach-side pool.

20 foot waterfall is also there.

2 clay tennis courts are at the Grand Floridan.

52 feet is the length of the Grand 1 yacht, available for charter cruises on Seven Seas Lagoon and Bay Lake.

11 original maps of Florida are in the gallery located near the entrance to Victoria & Albert's.

181 concierge accommodations are located at the resort.

Contemporary Resort

October, 24, 1971, is when the Contemporary opened.

55 acres were used for the resort.

555,417 square feet is its size.

9-ton rooms were constructed 3 miles away from the site and then installed like desk drawers.

70-foot tall Christmas tree is outside the Contemporary; it's the largest tree on property during the Christmas season.

35,000 white lights adorn the tree.

14 stories tall is the main tower.

1,057 total rooms were available on opening day.

394 of those rooms were in the tower.

663 were in the north and south garden wings.

6 dining spots were available on opening day: The Dock Inn, Grand Canyon Terrace, Gulf Coast Room, Mesa Grande Lounge, Pueblo Room, and Top of the World.

9 dining spots are available as of 2014: California Grill, Chef Mickey's, Contempo Cafe, Contemporary Grounds, Cove Bar, Outer Rim Lounge, Sand Bar, Top of the World, and The Wave.

8 shops were at the Contemporary on opening day.

3 buildings encompass the resort.

2 pools are there, with 1 designated a quiet pool.

90,000 feet of convention space is available.

$121,329,021.00 is the taxable value of the resort.

$38,808,000.00 is the land value.

$82,521,021.00 is the building value.

$1,699,848.70 in taxes was paid in 2006.

1,8000 hand-painted tiles are used in the mural in the Grand Canyon Concourse done by Mary Blair.

90-feet tall is the tiled mural in the Grand Canyon Concourse.

1.5 years were needed to complete the mural.

5-legged goat in the mural is best viewed from the 7th or 8th floors on the monorail side of the tower.

13 150-foot-long steel-trussed A-frames make up the structure.

17-foot-high spiraling slide is at the Contemporary Resort Pool.

15 rooms were completed on average per day during the initial construction.

$17,000 was the initial construction cost estimate per room; the actual amount was 5 times higher.

70 pounds of vine-ripened tomatoes are served every night during tomato season at the California Grill.

August 1, 2009, was opening day for Bay Lake Tower.

800 concrete piles were used as its foundation.

16 inches is the diameter of each of the concrete piles.

70 feet in ground is the depth of each concrete pile.

10 miles in the sky would be the height of all the piles used for Bay Lake Tower.

167 miles of post-tensioning cable are running through the concrete slabs. These cables could stretch from Bay Lake Tower to Disney's Vero Beach Resort and back.

1,398 tons of reinforcing steel were used.

15 stories is the height of Bay Lake Tower.

Boardwalk Inn & Villas

1996 is when the Boardwalk Inn & Villas opened.

45 acres were used to build the resort.

372 rooms are at the resort.

20 suites are available as well.

280-unit (2-bedroom equivalents) are located here.

20,000 square feet of convention space is available.

$43,320,003.00 is the taxable value of the resort.

$11,352,000.00 is the land value.

$31,968,003.00 is the building value.

$606,923.64 in taxes was paid in 2006.

9,000 square feet of shops and restaurants are here.

44 4-inch-tall horses, each unique in size and design, are on the mini-carousel in the lobby.

Disney's Yacht & Beach Club

1990 is when the Yacht Club opened.

65.44 acres were used for the Yacht & Beach Club resorts.

3 acres is the size of Stormalong Bay.

750,000 gallon pool and mini-water park, with water slide, sandy bottom, whirlpools, and water currents, are here.

25-acre Crescent Lake is here, too.

381 square feet is the size of a room that sleeps 4.

3 acres is the size of the swimming area.

2 kiddie pools are located here.

Yacht Club

621 rooms are at the Yacht Club.

73,000-square-foot convention center is available; it includes a 36,000-square-foot ballroom which seats up to 2,800 for dinner.

$39,501,000.00 is the taxable land value of the resort.

$107,863,275.00 is the building value.

$2,064,608.86 was paid in taxes in 2006.

Beach Club

576 rooms are at the Beach Club.

24-foot-high ceilings and natural French limestone floors are found in the lobby.

1927 Chevy Depot Wagon, or "Woody Huckster", is featured on the front porch of the Beach Club.

2,500 gallon freestanding saltwater aquarium was once featured here, the largest in the world.

Animal Kingdom Lodge

2001 is when the Animal Kingdom Lodge debuted.

972 rooms are available.

1 pool is here.

33-acre savanna features free roaming African animals.

3 separate savannas make up the entire acreage: Sunset, Arusha, and Uzima.

11,000 square foot pool area features a 67-foot-long water slide at Uzima.

100 sand live oak trees and 35,000 shrubs were planted in the savannas.

200 mammals and birds of nearly 3 dozen species populate the savannas.

6,000 square feet Zawadi Marketplace is one of the largest retail shops at a Disney World resort.

11,000 square feet pool area makes Uzima Springs one of the largest resort pools. It is also a "zero-depth entry" pool, meaning there is an entrance without steps.

67-foot long slide is at the pool.

234,980 gallons of water are needed to fill the pool.

150 seats are in the restaurant Sanaa and 24 people can sit in the adjacent bar.

Wilderness Lodge

1994 is when the Wilderness Lodge opened.

82-foot-tall fireplace and rocking chairs with hidden Mickey's, totem poles, wood carvings, teepee chandeliers, and other items are in the lobby.

7 floors are in the main building and 6 floors in the wing buildings.

3/4 mile wooded path is available for walking, jogging, or biking from Wilderness Lodge to Fort Wilderness.

120 foot in the air is how high the Wilderness Geyser shoots water every hour from 7am to 10pm.

727 rooms are in the resort.

344 square feet is the size of the room that sleeps 4 in 2 queen beds.

2 pools are at the Wilderness Lodge.

2 hot tubs are located here, too.

60 acres was used for the resort.

472,984 square feet is the size of the Wilderness Lodge.

750 square feet of meeting space is located here.

12-24-27-0000-00-002 is the parcel lot ID.

$87,832,671.00is the taxable value.

$24,024,000.00 is the land value.

$63,808,671.00 is the building value.

$1,230,556.80 was paid in taxes in 2006.

2 totem poles are in the lobby.

55 feet is the height of each totem pole.

4 massive chandeliers with glowing teepees on top of them are in the lobby.

1974 is when the Hoop-Dee-Doo Musical Revue began its first show, making it one of the longest running dinner shows in the world.

1976 to 1980 is when the Fort Wilderness Railroad was in service. The track were sinking and so the line had to shut down. One car became a ticket booth at Pleasure Island, and the others were sent to the Carolwood Pacific Historical Society.

4 tribal artifacts are represented in the lobby from the Cheyenne, Crow, Sioux and Blackfoot tribes.

Fort Wilderness

1974 is when Pioneer Hall opened.

1,283 hand-fitted pine logs from Montana were used to build the hall.

70 tons of stone from North Carolina were used as well.

Polynesian Village

1971 is when the Polynesian Village opened.

39 acres was used for the resort, which is styled as a South Pacific paradise, complete with beaches, tropical landscaping, waterfalls, and bamboo Tiki torches.

11 different buildings called longhouses contain the guest rooms.

16 cast members have stayed with the Polynesian since opening day, and the entire Polynesian cast represents about 1000 years of service at the resort. The Polynesian has one of the largest percentages of original cast members anywhere in Walt Disney World.

486 rooms are at the Polynesian resort (not including suites or DVC) as of 2015.

6 suites are available as of 2015.

484 rooms were at the Polynesian Village resort in 1971.

360 deluxe studios (DVC) were added in 2015.

20 2-bedroom, 2-bath over-the-water bungalows (DVC) were added in 2015.

6 dining spots were at the Polynesian Village in 1971.

10 dining spots are there now.

5 Shops were there on opening day.

12 stories was the original design.

2 pools are at the Polynesian; one is themed with a volcano and the other is not themed.

11-24-27-0000-00-007 is the parcel ID for this property.

$107,005,276.00 is the taxable value.

$32,609,500.00 is the land value.

$74,395,776.00 is the building value.

$1,499,169.59 was paid in taxes in 2006.

8,500 interior plants are used each year, the most of any Disney resort.

3,000 species of plants of used at the Polynesian, with a species from every continent except for Antarctica.

74 outrigger beams are atop the exterior.

42 feet above the roof line tower the outrigger beams.

415 square feet is the size of a room with 2 queens size beds.

2 hot tubs are located here.

1.5 mile walking trail starts at the Polynesian and continues to the Shades of Green resort.

1,000 lb Balinese Tiki statue is in the lobby.

35 years is how long Tonga Toast has been on the menu at the Polynesian.

1 "Kukui Nut" tree is located here; it's the only one of its kind in Florida.

2 is the number of stories the resort was going to be, according to the original concept drawings.

40 feet is the length of the war canoes that guests could rent on the Seven Seas Lagoon.

$1 was the cost to ride the Port O' Call, an excursion steamer that used to navigate the Seven Seas Lagoon and Bay Lake; kids could ride for $.50.

18 feet is the diameter of the fire pit at 'Ohana.

1,863 is the size of the 2-story King Kamehameha suite, making it one of the largest standard rooms on property.

Swan & Dolphin

1990 is when the Swan opened.

758 rooms are available.

52,000 square feet of convention space is also available.

1990 is when the Dolphin opened.

1,509 rooms are available.

202,000 square feet of convention space is also available.

Caribbean Beach

1988 is when the Caribbean Beach opened.

200 acres were used for this resort.

2,112 rooms are available.

314 square feet is the standard size of a room.

4 playgrounds are located here.

3 miles of roads encompass the resort.

6 villages are here: Barbados, Martinique, Aruba, Jamaica, Trinidad North, and Trinidad South.

45-acre lake, Barefoot Bay, is surrounded by a 1.4-mile promenade, which connects to winding paths leading to all guest rooms and common areas.

7 heated pools are here, including the Spanish fort-themed main pool at Old Port Royale (with water slide, water cannons, and waterfalls), the adjacent wading pool and whirlpool, and village pools.

82 feet is the length of the slide that goes though the Fuentes del Morro Fort and ends in the pool.

30-24-28-0000-00-002 is the parcel ID for this resort.

$151,485,450.00 is the taxable value.

$58,080,000.00 is the land value.

$93,405,450.00 is the building value.

$2,122,347.52 was paid in taxes in 2006.

Port Orleans

1991 is when Port Orleans opened.

325 acres were allocated to Port Orleans; 225 acres were developed.

1 kiddie pool is here.

5 quiet pools are also here.

Port Orleans—French Quarter

1,008 rooms are available at the French Quarter.

946 rooms have 2 double beds and 62 rooms have a king-size bed (with a higher room rate).

200-seat restaurant called Boatwright's Dining Hall is here.

314 square feet is the standard size of a room at Port Orleans.

1st verse of the song "When the Saints Come Marchin' In" is strung across the registration desk.

Port Orleans—Riverside

2,048 rooms available at Riverside.

314 square feet is the standard size of a room at Port Orleans.

512 rooms of Magnolia Bend were refinished in 2013.

2 million pounds of material was diverted from the landfill during the room rehab.

987,332 pounds of recyclable materials were sent to local recyclers for processing.

452,352 pounds were liquidated or donated to local charities.

147,456 pounds were salvaged, refinished, and then reused in guest rooms.

111,040 pounds of cardboard was diverted from the landfill.

91,767 pounds of metal was diverted from the landfill.

19,100 pounds of wood pallets was diverted from the landfill.

Coronado Springs

1997 is when Coronado Springs opened.

143.11 acres were used for this resort.

1,921 rooms are available.

95,000 square feet of convention space is also available, with a 60,214 square-foot ballroom.

5,000 people can be accommodated for a sit-down dinner or 6,500 meeting-style seats. There is also a 20,000 square-foot junior ballroom.

60 rooms have king-size beds; 1,718 have two double beds

1,181 non-smoking rooms and 99 disabled-accessible rooms are available, too.

400 guest can eat at the Pepper Market Food Court.

200-seat lounge called Francisco's offers specialty drinks and Southwestern-style snacks.

6,000 square-foot shop called Panchito's Gifts and Sundries is filled with Indian and Mestizo handicrafts and Disney's own character merchandise.

15-acre lake called Lago Dorado is here.

272,000 gallon pool called the Dig Site is here, too.

123-foot-long water slide (the Jaguar) is at the Dig Site.

3 quiet pools are here, at the Casitas, Ranchos, and Cabanas.

50-foot-tall Mayan pyramid is where you will find a themed pool as a modern archaeological site of a lost kingdom.

25-24-27-0000-00-020 is the parcel ID of Coronado Springs.

$153,390,352.00 is the taxable value.

$49,946,000.00 is the land value.

$103,444,352.00 is the building value.

$2,149,035.65 was paid in taxes in 2006.

Disney's All-Star Resorts

246 acres was set aside for the three All-Star resorts: Sports, Movies, Music.

8640 rooms are available at these three resorts.

23,556 guests can stay in these rooms.

260 square feet is the size of the All-Star rooms (the smallest, and least expensive, on property).

All Star Music

1994 is when All-Star Music opened.

4,000 CDs would be needed to fill the jukebox in the "Rock Inn" area of the resort. That is enough music to play for 135 days without listening to the same CD twice.

160,000 gallons of water are needed to fill the piano pool.

All-Star Sports

1994 is when All-Star Sports opened.

31-feet high are the goalie nets that surround the stair-wells at the Mighty Ducks buildings.

20 million 12-ounce cans of Coke could fit in the Coke cup.

9,474,609 tennis balls would be needed to fill one of the tennis ball cans at Center Court Hotel.

12 surfboards surround the pool.

2 38 foot shark fins circle the pool.

60 feet long and 20 feet high is the size of the whistles.

9 feet is the diameter of the whistle pea inside the whistles.

200 feet tall is how tall a player would have be to wear the giant football helmet

All Star Movies

1999 is when All-Star Movies debuted.

231,610 gallons of water are needed to fill the Fantasia pool.

5 times his normal size is the Herbie Love bug car.

40-foot tall Pongo and 35-foot tall Perdita are at the 101 Dalmatians building.

35-foot tall Buzz Lightyear and a 25-foot tall Woody with Green Army Men are on top of the Toy Story building.

Pop Century

2003 is when Pop Century opened.

5,760 rooms are available.

177 acres encompasses the resort.

16 miles of railing are here.

2.5 acres of window surface need to be cleaned.

14 acres of roofing are at this resort.

36.5 acres of carpet and over 230,000 gallons of paint were used.

260 square feet is the size of a Pop Century room with 2 double beds.

3 swimming pools are available.

4 stories is the height of a building at Pop Century.

41-foot-high Rubik's cube is here.

65-foot-high bowling pins are here, too.

9 of these pins are located at the resort (the 10th is the bowling pin in the courtyard).

35 feet tall are the 8-track tapes, with "tape" that is more than 1 foot in width. A real 8-track tape is a mere 5¼ inches tall, with ¼ inch wide tape.

12 feet tall are the soccer players, and the "toy" ball is more than 2½ feet in diameter.

51 display cases are in the lobby holding various pop culture artifacts.

33 acres on the other side of the lake are available for the "Legendary Years" buildings for the decades from 1900 to 1940.

0 pool slides are here.

4 giant flowers at the pool sprinkle water.

877 pounds would be the weight of a person big enough to ride the giant Big Wheel.

5,000-square-foot retail center is in Classic Hall.

125,000 gallons of paint were used to create the bright colors and tie-dyed hues on the buildings' interior and exterior walls.

10 buildings make up this resort, not including the main lobby.

4 story jukebox can be found in the 1950s buildings.

30-foot-tall Mickey Mouse Phone can be seen (but not used).

Art of Animation

864 standard rooms are available.

1164 family suite rooms are available, too.

600 rooms will have balconies.

310,000 gallons of water are in the Big Blue pool, the largest pool at Disney World; it has an underwater speaker system, too.

1,224 ft is how high the pile would be if you stacked all the doors used at the resort (as high as the Empire State Building).

27 acres of landscaping is here (equivalent to 20 football fields).

77 animation sketches are displayed at the resort and used in the lobby chandelier.

2,500 sculpted figures are here.

2,200 square feet is the size of the Landscape of Flavors food court.

600 guests can be seated there.

4 locations in the food court have hidden Mickeys.

11 of the characters from *Cars* can be found at the resort.

1st time ever at any Disney resort hotel, in-room décor pieces may be purchased at the gift shop, for example, the "Bruce" shower curtain or cozy cone lamps.

1st time ever a Disney value resort has a business center.

800 construction jobs were created to build this resort.

87 acres is the total land used.

2,300 parking spaces are available.

125 cars could be parked inside all the swimming pools.

23,000 gallons of paint were used (enough to fill a typical backyard swimming pool).

529,000 square feet of ceramic tiles were used (enough to cover a standard 2-lane road 4 miles long).

40 animation sketches make up the character development wall that spans Animation Hall from the check-in area to the arcade.

4,500 square foot arcade area is in Animation Hall.

Old Key West

1991 is when Old Key West opened.

531 units are available.

376 square feet is the size of a studio villa.

942 square feet is the size of a 1 bedroom villa.

1,333 square feet is the size of a 2 bedroom villa.

2,202 square feet is the size of a 3 bedroom villa.

4 swimming pools are located here.

4 hot tubs are here.

2 arcades are here.

3 lighted tennis courts are here.

4 playgrounds are here as well.

Saratoga Springs Resort & Spa

2004 is when Disney's Saratoga Springs Resort & Spa opened.

65 acres were used for the resort.

18 villa buildings make up the resort.

828 rooms are available.

365 square feet is the size of a studio villa.

714 square feet is the size of a 1 bedroom villa.

1,075 square feet is the size of a 2 bedroom villa.

2,113 square feet is the size of a grand villa.

60 treehouse villas are available as well.

10 feet off the ground is each treehouse villa.

2007 is when Saratoga Springs Resort & Spa entered the Florida Green Lodging Program.

4 swimming pools are located here.

4 hot tubs are here.

3 lighted tennis courts are here.

2 playgrounds are here.

65.22% of the materials used to construct the treehouse villas came from recycled materials.

480 concrete columns are used to support all 60 of these villas.

87,858 lineal feet, or 16.6 miles, of wire for fiber optics, copper, telephones, and CATV were used in the construction of the villas.

5,178 tons of materials from demolition done in 2008 were recycled, including concrete and metals.

Walt Disney World Dining

1,200 people eat at Chef Mickey's everyday.

4,000 eggs are served there each day.

1,700 Mickey-shaped waffles are served there each day.

1,500 pancakes are served there each day.

1 restaurant on property has received the exclusive AAA Five Diamond Award: Victoria's & Albert's at the Grand Floridian.

8,000 recipes are on file throughout all the eateries at Walt Disney World.

125 orders of meatloaf and mashed potatoes are requested every single day at the 50s Prime Time Cafe at Disney's Hollywood Studio.

70 pounds of tomatoes are served at the California Grill every night during tomato season, which is July through November.

6 million hot dogs are consumed each year at Disney World.

1.6 million barbecued turkey legs are consumed there each year.

40–50 pounds is the average size of the turkey used to make them.

1.5 lbs is the average weight of each turkey leg.

6 hours is needed to cook it.

3 million pizzas are sold each year.

1,200 pizzas are made each hour using custom-made pizza makers.

2 oz sauce, 3 oz cheese, and 4–6 oz of pepperoni are used on each pizza.

4–5 minutes are needed to make each pizza.

1,200 pounds of ribs are smoked at one time at the Flame Tree BBQ in Animal Kingdom.

.5 million pounds of macaroni and cheese are consumed each year.

5 pastry chefs are assigned just to make wedding cakes.

350+ chefs work at Walt Disney World.

1 million pounds of watermelon are used each year.

5 million servings of popcorn are consumed each year.

322,000 pounds of popcorn are popped every year.

2,000 people dine at Chef Mickey's each day.

18 tables are available at Victoria & Albert's.

5 tables are in its fireplace room.

7-course custom menu is served there.

13 workers are in the kitchen.

13 courses are served at the chef's table inside the kitchen.

4 hours are needed to eat at the chef's table.

700 selections are on the wine list.

4,200 selections are in the wine cellar.

700+ sommeliers have been awarded the Court of Master Sommelier Introductory Certificate.

300+ sommeliers currently work in Disney World restaurants.

10,000 dessert soufflés a year come out of the oven at Victoria & Albert's.

30 tons of fruits and vegetables grown in The Land Pavilion at Epcot are served in Disney World restaurants.

720 pounds of pasta are served every day at Mama Melrose's Ristorante Italiano at Disney's Hollywood Studio.

89 varieties of cheese are used by Disney theme park and resort chefs.

400,000 pounds of unused, prepared food is donated annually through the Disney Harvest program to feed the homeless of central Florida.

26.2 miles of bratwurst are served every 60 days at the Biergarten restaurant in the Germany Pavilion at Epcot.

190 guests can dine at Big River Grille & Brewing Company.

450 guests can be seated at the ESPN Club.

193 guests can be seated at the Flying Fish Cafe.

205 guests can be seated at Spoodles.

132 guests can be seated at Shutters.

500 guests can be seated at the Caribbean Beach's Centertown food court.

156 guests can be seated at the California Grill.

405 guests can be seated at Chef Mickey's.

222 guests can be seated at the Wave.

220 guest can be seated at the Maya Grill.

420 guests can be seated at the Pepper Market.

192 guests can be seated at Trail's End Restaurant.

360 guests can be seated at the Hoop-Dee-Doo Musical Revue.

300 guests can be seated at Mickey's Backyard Barbecue.

270 guests can be seated at 1900 Park Fare.

190 guests can be seated at Citricos.

326 guests can be seated at Grand Floridian Cafe.

270 guests can be seated at Narcoosee's.

90 guests can be seated at Victoria & Albert's.

150 guests can be seated at the Grand Floridian's Gasparilla Grill and Games.

156 guests can be seated at Olivia's Cafe, and 22 more outside.

162 guests can be seated at Kona Cafe.

300 guests can be seated at 'Ohana.

420 guests can be seated at Spirit of Aloha.

650 guests can eat at the Everything POP food court.

206 guests can be seated at Boatwright's Dining Hall.

550 guests can be seated at the Riverside Mill food court.

550 guests can be seated at Sassagoula Floatworks & Food Factory.

146 guests can be seated at the Turf Club Bar & Grill.

112 guests can be seated at The Artist's Palette.

235 Guests can be seat at Artist Point.

281 Guests can be seated at Whispering Canyon Cafe.

250 guests can be seated at Roaring Fork Snacks.

48 guests can be seated at Beaches & Cream.

234 guests can be seated at Cape May Cafe.

280 guests can be seated at the Captain's Grill.

286 guests can be seated at Yachtsman Steakhouse.

800 pounds of ribs are served at the Hoop-Dee-Doo Musical Revue each night.

3.3 million chocolate-covered Mickey Mouse ice cream bars are sold each year at Disney World.

9.7 million hamburgers are sold each year.

5.8 million hot dogs are sold each year.

9 million pounds of French fries are sold each year.

18.2 million ketchup packets are used each year.

2 million pounds of bulk ketchup are used each year.

50 million soft drinks are sold each year.

319,353 pounds of chocolate are used each year.

741,150 pounds of sugar are used each year.

1.8 million pounds of flour are used each year.

245,000 pounds of fruit filling are used each year.

38,000 pounds of white icing glaze are used each year.

2.9 million pounds of eggs are used each year.

606,000 pounds of bananas are used each year.

510,000 pounds of grapes are used each year.

1.5 million soft pretzels are served each year.

2,000 slices of apple strudel are served each year.

1980 is when the Mickey bar first appeared in the parks.

8,100 Mickey bars are made per hour at the Nestle factory near Fresno, California.

170,000 Mickey bars are made there per day.

100 Mickey bars are formed per minute.

12 minutes are need to freeze a Mickey bar.

-60 degrees is the temperature at which the Mickey bars are frozen.

3,000 servings of rice cream are made from 1 daily batch.

9 gallons of water go into it.

40 pounds of rice go into it.

9 gallons of milk go into it as well.

1 million servings of rice cream are served each year at Disney World.

20 tons of fresh fruits and vegetables are consumed there each year.

Walt Disney World Recreation

6 golf courses are located at Disney World: Eagle Pines, Osprey Ridge, Lake Buena Vista, Palm, Magnolia, and Oak Trail.

99 holes of golf are available at these courses.

2 miniature golf courses are located at Disney World: Winter Summerland and Fantasia Gardens.

25 resort tennis courts are available throughout the property.

200 acres of Disney's Wide World of Sports complex offers 11 lighted, world-class clay tennis courts. The center court stadium has permanent seating for 1,100 and was host to the men's Clay Court Championships from 1997–2000.

9,500-seat baseball stadium is located there as well.

5,000-seat field house at the complex is the official spring training home of the Atlanta Braves.

250,000 athletes visit Disney's Wide World of Sports each year.

1.2 million spectator and fans visit each year as well.

1.5 mile jogging trail is at Fort Wilderness and Wilderness Lodge.

1.4 mile jogging trail is at the Caribbean Beach.

2 jogging trails are at Port Orleans.

Fantasia Gardens

40-foot-tall Mount Olympus complete with waterfalls is at Fantasia Gardens.

11 acres is the size of the course.

4 holes ranging in length from 40 to 75 feet are available.

21,060 sq feet of open air pavilions and meeting space is adjacent to Fantasia Gardens.

Disney's Wide World of Sports

105 acres of Tifway 419 Bermuda sports turf is here, enough to sod an entire 18-hole golf course.

5-7 inches or more of rainfall per hour can be removed from the playable fields due to an efficient drainage system.

750,000 tons of orange grove sand was imported and spread throughout the property during the first stage of its construction.

26 miles of electrical conduit and fiber optics technology is at Wide World of Sports.

4 sporting events can be broadcast simultaneously.

2-decker spring training baseball stadium is the tallest in the state.

21 inches wide are the seats at the ballpark, the roomiest in the industry.

80 percent of the seats are in prime viewing areas between first and third base.

83 feet high are the trusses in the Milk House (fieldhouse), reminiscent of 1950s-style architecture.

3,000-square-foot weight room can be used by every athlete at the complex.

2 of the largest air conditioners at Disney World cool the Milk House.

2 Data Tracking Network weather stations provide up-to-the-minute information about storms and other meteorological activity that could affect play.

35,000 compete in Disney's Endurance Series, which include marathons and other events.

3,000 basketball games are scheduled at Disney's Wide World of Sports each year.

2,400 softball games are scheduled each year.

1,800 baseball games are scheduled each year.

3,900 soccer matches are scheduled each year.

Walt Disney World Transportation

Railroad

4 trains are part of the Walt Disney Railroad: *Walter E. Disney* (red), *Lilly Belle* (green), *Roger E. Broggie* (yellow), and *Roy O. Disney* (blue).

5 passenger cars are on each train.

360 guests (and 2 wheelchairs) is the capacity of each train.

10 miles per hour is the touring speed of the trains.

1.5 mile grand-circle tour of Disney World takes about 20 minutes.

1.5 million guests ride the railroad each year.

7 cars make a complete train set: 1 locomotive, and 1 tender, and 5 passenger cars.

1,837 gallons of water are carried in the tender.

664 gallons of fuel is also carried.

2 or 3 trips is the limit before the tender needs to topped off with water.

1925 is when the *Walter E. Disney* was built.

4-6-0 is its wheel configuration.

58444 is its serial number.

44 inches is its drive wheel diameter.

67,000 pounds is the dry weight of its locomotive and tender.

1928 is when the *Lilly Belle* was built.

2-6-0 is its wheel configuration.

44 inches is its drive wheel diameter.

61,000 pounds is the dry weight of its locomotive and tender.

1925 is when the *Roger E. Broggie* was built.

4-6-0 is its wheel configuration.

44 inches is its drive wheel diameter.

67,000 pounds is the dry weight of its locomotive and tender.

1916 is when the *Roy O Disney* was built.

4-4-0 is its wheel configuration.

42915 is its serial number.

46 inches is its drive wheel diameter.

51,000 pounds is the dry weight of its locomotive and tender.

3 cast members man each train, a conductor, an engineer, and a fireman.

4 sets of passengers cars are in service: red, yellow, blue, and green. The green cars only appear during the park opening, as they are missing the safety rails on the left (this is so cast members can exit on the left during the opening show).

1 bridge near Frontierland is part of a 2-lane bridge from the original Florida Flagler Route.

Monorail

50 million guests use the monorail each year, making it the busiest monorail system in the world.

150,000 guests use the monorail system per day.

14.7 miles is the total beam length, which covers 2 theme parks, 3 resorts and 1 parking lot.

337 individual track beams were used on the original monorail loop that consisted of the resort hotels and Magic Kingdom.

3 monorails were in operation on opening day in 1971 (orange, green, and gold).

$1,000,000 per mile was the estimated cost to build the monorail system.

12 Mark VI monorails trains are in service, each identified by a color: peach, teal, red, coral, orange, gold, yellow, lime, green, blue, silver, and black. Purple has been retired.

6 cars make up each monorail train.

203 feet, 6 inches is the overall length of a Mark VI monorail.

10 feet, 10.5 inches is its height.

124 tires are on each monorail.

300–372 guests are the capacity.

4,200 feet of track was originally installed, and has been expanded since then.

50 mph is the maximum speed of the monorail, but they typically don't exceed 40 mph.

10 selections are on the monorail Master Control Unit (MCU): 5 forward, 1 center, and 4 back.

5 forward positions are propulsion selections labeled P-1 through P-5. They correspond to speed traveled: P-1 = 15

mph, P-2 = 20 mph, P-3 = 25 mph, P-4 = 30 mph, P-5 = 40 mph.

4 back positions are labeled B-1 to B-4. They correspond to breaking; the higher the number, the harder the brakes.

1 center position is neutral.

8 electric motors are on each monorail.

113 horsepower is delivered from each motor.

600 volts of DC power is generated from each motor.

99.9% up time for the monorail system. Each train has a strict maintenance schedule.

26 inches is the width of the monorail track.

77,427 feet is the total track length.

65 feet is the highest point of the track.

400 beams were used to construct the original track.

110 feet long is each section (beam) of track.

200 pilots operate the monorail system.

2009 was the first time in the 48-year history of the monorail that there was a fatal accident.

1 death occurred at 2am on July 5, 2009, as a result of a head on collision of 2 monorails: a 21-year-old monorail pilot, Austin Wuennenberg, died at the scene of the accident at the TTC.

9/1/71 is when Monorail Orange was put into service.

9/1/71 is when Monorail Green was put into service.

9/1/71 is when Monorail Gold was put into service.

9/20/71 is when Monorail Blue was put into service.

11/7/71 is when Monorail Red was put into service.

12/3/71 is when Monorail Yellow was put into service.

7/3/72 is when Monorail Pink was put into service.

8/16/72 is when Monorail Silver was put into service.

11/14/72 is when Monorail Purple was put into service.

12/22/72 is when Monorail Black was put into service.

Mousecellaneous

100 tons of laundry is processed at Walt Disney World each day.

1.4 million pounds of laundry per week is processed.

32,000 costumes are laundered each day.

8 million pounds of food and beverage linen are cleaned annually.

132,000 square feet is the size of the laundry plant in the north service area. It's one of the largest, completely automated, state-of-the-art laundry plants in the world.

60–62 megawatts on average are consumed at Disney World each day.

28,000 square feet is the size of the Materials Recovery Facility, which processes over 30 tons per day of recyclable materials, including cardboard, paper, steel, aluminum, glass, and plastic.

96 times taller than Cinderella Castle is how high all the buttons used by the Costuming Plant Seam Team in one year would stack.

200 times taller than Cinderella Castles is how high all the standard autograph books sold in 1 year would stack.

88 miles into space is how high all the Princess-style autograph books would reach if stacked end-to-end.

340 acres is the size of Bay Lake.

230 buses transport guests around property, making the Disney World fleet the third largest fleet in Florida behind those of Miami and Jacksonville.

2 million calls are handled each month by Disney's own telecommunication company, Vista-United.

1971 is when Vista-United installed the first 911 emergency system in Florida.

1978 is when Vista-United installed the first commercial fiber-optic system.

4.8 million calls are handled by Central Reservation Operations (CRO) each year.

600 cast members work in CRO during the peak season.

150 outfits are available for Mickey Mouse to wear, ranging from a tuxedo to scuba gear.

200 outfits are available for Minnie Mouse, ranging from a gown to a cheerleading outfit.

75 million Cokes are consumed each year at Disney World.

13 million bottles of water are consumed.

MyMagic+

7 colors are used for the bands: red, blue, green, pink, yellow, orange, and grey.

800,000 guests participated in the beta testing period of MyMagic+ testing.

10,000 cast members participated, too.

600,000 bands were customized during beta testing.

17 million payment transactions were processed.

1 color was the most popular (pink), followed by blue, green, red, gray, and yellow.

Horticulture

2,000 acres of grass must be cut at Disney World.

50,000 pine trees were planted by cast members across 50 acres to form a "hidden Mickey" in honor of the park's 20th anniversary on February 27, 1992.

7,500 acres were set-aside as conservation area in 1970, with a system of more than 43 miles of canals and 22 miles of levees to control the water level.

7 million trees, shrubs, and plants are at Disney World.

2 million shrubs are planted there annually.

13,000 roses are planted annually (400 hours are needed to remove the spent rose bulbs).

200+ or so topiary are used throughout the park.

20 different plants, flowers, mosses, and lichens are used to make 1 topiary.

4,200 acres are devoted to maintained landscapes and gardens.

800 hanging baskets of flowers and plants are used throughout Disney World.

50–75 4" plants are used to create 1 poinsettia ball.

3 months are needed to grow each poinsettia plant.

3 months on stage is the total time for each poinsettia ball.

2,000 acres of turf need to be maintained.

3 mowings a week are needed to keep the turf well groomed.

450,000 miles of mowing are done each year.

18 trips around the equator would equal all the mowing done at Disney World each year.

190 acres in the south service area, in the southwest corner of the property, is the nursery complex.

8,000 trees were in the original tree farm inventory.

60,000 plants were acquired, moved, acclimated, and transplanted by 1970.

800 different varieties of trees were acquired, moved, acclimated, and transplanted, as well.

1,000,000 trees, plants, and shrubs are at Disney World.

100,000 trees have been planted since the opening of the Magic Kingdom in 1971.

50,000 sprinkler heads are in use.

2,000 miles of irrigation pipe are also in use.

3,500 acres of landscaping are maintained.

2 million tended shrubs have been planted since 1971.

1,700 species of plants are used.

50 countries have plant species at Disney World.

12% of the property (nearly 3,000 football fields, or about 4,000 acres) is devoted to gardens and maintained landscapes.

3 million bedding plants and annuals are planted each year.

8,500 interior plants are planted each year.

100-acre "browse farm" is used to replace natural forage like acacia, hibiscus, and mulberry, which is fed to the animals at the Animal Kingdom.

10.5 million beneficial insects are released each year to control plant pests.

600 horticulture professionals, gardeners, arborists, irrigation specialists, and pest management specialists are employed at Disney World.

Reedy Creek Improvement District

15 miles southwest of Orlando is the Reedy Creek Improvement District (RCID).

25,000 acres or 38.6 square miles encompasses the district.

18,800 acres are located in Orange County; 6,200 acres are in Osceola County.

2 cities are in the district: Lake Buena Vista and Bay Lake.

6 ambulances provide advanced life support service and are staffed with paramedics qualified to perform multiple procedures.

40 stand-alone personal computers powered the original Reedy Creek technology network

200+ PCs now power the network.

23 water control structures and 47 miles of canals with 22 miles of levees were built and are maintained by the Reedy Creek Planning and Engineering Department.

113 lane-miles of roadways are in the district.

300 full-time employees are employed by RCID.

731 elevators and escalators are inspected every six months.

40,050 permits and 1,650 certificates of occupancy have been issued since 1969 by RCID.

1,500 structures are fire-inspected each year.

450 commercial kitchens are inspected weekly.

500,000 fireworks shells are fired annually within the boundaries of RCID.

5,475 alarm points are monitored by the communication center operated by RCID.

5 million gallons of water per day is used for irrigation of golf courses and other landscaped areas.

15 million gallons per day of waste water is processed through a tertiary treatment plant.

11 Floridian aquifer wells and four pump stations with a total design rating of 60 million gallons per day meet an average daily demand of 14 million gallons of water.

5 above-ground water storage tanks with a combined capacity of 7.95 million gallons help meet demand during peak periods.

3,000 sensors detect unusual water flow to help control flooding.

813,000 pounds of packing material is saved each year by Disney purchasing jumbo rolls of toilet paper and paper towels.

263,085 pounds of waste was saved each year by reducing the napkin dispensers by 25%.

1 million pounds of broken wood, surplus wood, and shipping pallets are collected and ground into garden mulch each year.

50 million gallons of water are saved each year by the toilet and sink sensors.

700 tons of food scraps are used each year as livestock feed and even more is composted.

29 million gallons of water are saved each year though a new laundry process (enough water to fill the aquarium at The Seas with Nemo and Friends 6 times).

61,000 therms of natural gas is saved annually by this new process (enough to power 1452 household clothes dryers for one year).

194,000 incandescent light bulbs were replaced in 2009 with compact fluorescent bulbs that use roughly ¼ of the energy of traditional light bulbs.

26 million kilowatt hours are saved annually by switching to fluorescent bulbs (enough electricity to power 1450 homes for one year).

430,000 incandescent holiday lights were converted to LEDs, saving an estimated 1.1 million kilowatt hours throughout the holiday season (enough to power 61 homes for one year).

85% of the hot water used by guests at the Pop Century is from a prototype system developed by Disney engineers to recover excess heat from rooftop air conditioner units during the summer months. This saves 11,500 therms each year (enough to provide hot water to 151 homes).

6 million gallons of reclaimed water is captured each day and used to irrigate the landscape, wash buses, and clean streets (enough to fill 400 home swimming pools each day for a year).

150,000 reusable bags have been purchased by WDW , resulting in approximately $50,000 raised for the Disney Worldwide Conservation Fund.

8,500 acres of the Walker Ranch was purchased by the Disney Wilderness Preserve in April 1993.

170 tons of waste is generated each day at Disney World, of which about 55 tons is recycled.

3,252 tons of food waste is collected by a local pig farmer as feed.

Magic Kingdom
Holiday Decorations

26 feet wide is the width of the Christmas tree used in Magic Kingdom.

65-foot Christmas tree is erected in the center of Main Street each Christmas season.

7-ton crane is used to position the theme park Christmas trees into place each year.

25,000 poinsettias are used to decorate the Magic Kingdom for the holidays.

2 nights are needed and a crew of 30 people to do the holiday theming.

200,000 LED dream lights adorn the castle.

500 strobes are used to create the sparkling lighting effect.

32,000 square feet of fish netting is used hang the LED lights on the Castle.

15 miles of cable are used to hang all the lights.

Epcot Holiday Decorations

11 countries are dressed for Holidays Around the World at World Showcase.

30,000 lights are used on the Lights of Winter display canopy as you enter World Showcase.

65-foot tree is on display at Epcot each Christmas season.

800 performers are used each night during the Candlelight Processional.

200 guest choirs perform over the course of the processionals.

Best Friends Pet Care Resort

2010 is when Best Friends Pet Care Resort opened.

27,000-square-foot is the total space used for the facility.

270 dogs of all breeds and sizes can be kenneled here at once.

30 cats can be accommodated at the Kitty City pavilion with two- and four-story cat condos.

3,300-square-foot play area is covered in artificial turf.

4,500-square-foot area is dotted with shade trees for owners who want to sit and watch pets play.

1,300-square-foot splash-and-shake zone is available.

2 1,100-square-foot doggy day-camp rooms open onto their own play yards.

Disney's Wedding Pavilion

1995 is when the Wedding Pavilion opened.

4.75 acres are used for the pavilion.

$2,727,526.00 is its taxable value.

$1,594,781.00 is the land value.

$999,805.00 is the building value.

$38,213.29 was paid in taxes in 2006.

6 weddings a day can be conducted.

$20,000 is the average cost of a wedding for 50 people.

1st wedding at the pavilion was televised live June 18, 1995, on the Lifetime channel.

2 times during the 15-year history of the Walt Disney World Marathon couples have stopped mid-race to get married in front of Cinderella Castle.

2,000 decorative wedding cakes a year are made for couples exchanging vows.

300 soon-to-be-grooms popped the question at Cinderella's Royal Table in 2009.

1,600 couples tie the knot each year at Disney World.

10,000 couples honeymoon there each year.

Disclaimer

Given the thousands of numbers in this book, some are bound to be wrong. The numbers change over time, and reasonable people may differ over whether Disney actually does use 730,102 gallons of bleach every year, or whether it's 730,103 gallons, or even 729,687 gallons.

Although the author sourced much of the information from Disney itself, we're pretty sure that Mickey's bean counters are okay with a slight margin of error in bleach, and in other things as well.

The only thing we couldn't quantify was the pixie dust, as that seems infinite.

Acknowledgments

First and foremost, I want to acknowledge Walter Elias "Walt" Disney for building the first "theme park".

I also want to acknowledge:

The Imagineers, cast members, designers, and workers that help to bring the Disney parks to life;

Michael Eisner and Bob Iger for providing leadership to the Disney Company;

John Lasseter, Edwin Catmull, Alvy Ray Smith, and Steve Jobs for creating Pixar;

Bob McLain for publishing this book;

And last but not least, the followers and fans of, and contributors to, my website, DisneyByTheNumb3rs.com, and the listeners, co-hosts, and guests who have supported DisneyParksPodcast.com.

About the Author

My enthusiasm for all things Disney started when my parents took our family to Walt Disney World. My first trip was at age thirteen, and it's when my fascination with the park began. I wanted to know how things there worked. I wanted details about such things as the number of cast members and the length of the monorail track. Each visit brought new information.

Later, after my family moved to Orlando and I graduated from college, I got a job at Disney World as a security cast member. My four duties were driving a security vehicle, standing a post, working in a resort, and walking a park or other area. Sometimes I even had special duties like working the Epcot Candlelight Processional. I would also escort celebrity guests from backstage into the park.

As a cast member, I was given a little book of facts that I could reference when answering questions from guests. The facts in that book form the backbone of the facts in this book. I added many, many facts to what I already knew, and organized them all in a spreadsheet. Not long after, I started a website called Disney by the Numb3rs, and now that website—or parts of it, anyway—has become a book.

More Books from Theme Park Press

Theme Park Press publishes dozens of books each year for Disney fans and for general and academic audiences. Here are just a few of our titles. For the complete catalog, including book descriptions and excerpts, please visit:

ThemeParkPress.com

Death in the Tragic Kingdom

An Unauthorized Walking Tour Through the Haunted and Fatal History of Disney Parks

Keaton Moll

EVERYTHING I KNOW I LEARNED FROM DISNEY ANIMATED FEATURE FILMS

Advice for Living Happily Ever After

JIM KORKIS
Author of The Vault of Walt

A Disney Historian FUN FACT Book

A Historical Tour of Walt Disney World

Jungle Cruise

Pirates of the Caribbean

Enchanted TIKI Room

Crystal Palace

Main Street, U.S.A.

Carousel of Progress

Tomorrowland

VOLUME I

ANDREW KISTE

THE DISNEYLAND RAILROAD

A Complete History in Words and Pictures

Steve DeGaetano
Illustrations by Preston Nirattisai

From **Jungle Cruise Skipper** to Disney Legend

40 Years of Magical Memories at Disney

William "Sully" Sullivan

Katie

EARNS
HER EARS

My Secret Walt Disney World
Cast Member Diary

KATIE HUDSON
Earning Your Ears: Volume Four

MURDER
IN THE MAGIC KINGDOM

Annie Salisbury

Walt Disney
AND THE PROMISE OF
Progress City

SAM GENNAWEY
Foreword by Werner Weiss

32304608R00092

Made in the USA
Middletown, DE
30 May 2016